Information Privacy Fundamentals for Librarians and Information Professionals

Information Privacy Fundamentals for Librarians and Information Professionals

Cherie L. Givens

ROWMAN & LITTLEFIELD
Lanham • Boulder • New York • London

Published by Rowman & Littlefield
A wholly owned subsidary of The Rowman & Littlefield Publishing Group, Inc.
4501 Forbes Boulevard, Suite 200, Lanham, Maryland 20706
www.rowman.com

Unit A, Whitacre Mews, 26-34 Stannery Street, London SE11 4AB, United Kingdom

British Library Cataloguing in Publication Information Available

Library of Congress Cataloging-in-Publication Data

Givens, Cherie L., 1969-
Information privacy fundamentals for librarians and information professionals / Cherie L. Givens.
p. cm.
Includes bibliographical references and index.
ISBN 978-1-4422-4211-1 (cloth : alk. paper) — ISBN 978-1-4422-2881-8 (pbk. : alk. paper) —
ISBN 978-1-4422-2882-5 (ebook)
1. Records—Access control—United States. 2. Data protection—Law and legislation—United
States. 3. Computer security—Law and legislation—United States. 4. Privacy, Right of—United
States. 5. Library legislation—United States. 6. Information services—Law and legislation—United
States. I. Title.
KF1263.C65G58 2015
025.5—dc23
2014023397

∞™ The paper used in this publication meets the minimum requirements of American
National Standard for Information Sciences Permanence of Paper for Printed Library
Materials, ANSI/NISO Z39.48-1992.

Printed in the United States of America

This book is intended for informational purposes only. It should not be used as legal advice. Readers should consult an attorney for advice regarding specific legal questions and the laws that apply to their unique work environments. Privacy professionals should be consulted by those seeking assistance creating privacy policies, programs, and training as well as performing assessments and audits.

Table of Contents

Acknowledgments

This book would not have been possible without the encouragement, friendship, and assistance of many people. Special thanks are owed to Hank for his enduring support of this endeavor. I thank Eric Moskowitz and Bertha Ochoa for their assistance in editing and preparing this manuscript.

I owe special thanks to the International Association of Privacy Professionals and many of the members of this wonderful group for inspiring me to develop my expertise in the field of information privacy. I appreciate the supportive environment and many learning opportunities that have been made available to me through Privacy Summits, KnowledgeNets, and thoughtful conversations.

I am grateful to Mary Alice Baish, Superintendent of Documents, U.S. Government Printing Office, for providing me with the opportunity to develop privacy policies and procedures, serve as privacy point of contact, and address privacy matters for the Office of the Superintendent of Documents and the Library Services and Content Management business unit. My work at the U.S. Government Printing Office inspired this book.

Special thanks are owed to my editor, Charles Harmon, for suggesting that I write a book about information privacy, giving me the opportunity to do so, and shepherding me along the way. I thank everyone at Rowman & Littlefield who helped to bring this book to press.

Preface

I wrote this book to help educate librarians and information science professionals about the fundamentals of information privacy. When I worked in library services and content management for the federal government, I had the opportunity to see firsthand that information privacy issues occur in the workplace and that those working in library and information positions can find themselves on the front lines, needing to be able to identify and address these issues. *Information Privacy Fundamentals for Librarians and Information Professionals* is designed to provide an introduction to information privacy laws and practices while incorporating practical privacy information for those who will need to identify and address privacy issues in the workplace.

As information science programs diversify, they provide a broader range of career paths and training for students who will work in increasingly diverse work environments. Many students will find employment outside of the traditional library and school environments. They may work in positions in government, businesses, and health care environments. It is crucial that those in the information professions understand what laws and regulations govern the handling of personally identifiable information (PII) in their work environments and be able to identify information privacy issues and address them.

It is my firm belief that if those of us working in the information professions do not fully embrace information privacy, others will decide our privacy policies and practices. We manage information. Personal data, also known as PII, is a form of information. Becoming proficient in applying the laws, regulations, and best practices for managing personal data is a necessary part of the educational process.

Information privacy is a growing and changing field. No one book can teach you everything you need to know. This book is designed to provide readers with a foundation that reflects current law and practice on which to build their privacy knowledge. Laws change, practices change, and professionals must continue to educate themselves to keep abreast of those changes. Everyone needs to know how to protect personal data in their professional and personal lives.

It is presumed that this book will be read cover to cover or referred to by chapter for quick reviews. Read it completely for an understanding of the fundamentals of information privacy from a library and information science perspective. Use this book as a reference and consult relevant chapters for specific areas of interest. I have included references where needed to aid those who seek to use this book as a reference only. Some redundancy was necessary to allow for the use of this book as a chapter- and topic-specific reference.

Chapter One

Introduction to Information Privacy

Issues surrounding information privacy have gained prominence in recent years due to changes in technology and the rise of data mining. The increasing ability and efforts to gather data about individuals—including information about their health, finances, and online activities—have increased privacy concerns. Continuing reports of data breaches, secret data collections, deceptive privacy policies, and large-scale spying and data collection have made us a country weary of the efforts of companies, governments, and enterprising individuals to collect and analyze our private information. Concerns about information privacy are increasing globally. Americans' rising concerns about information privacy are evident in a July 2013 Pew report[1] that examines attitudes about the National Security Agency (NSA) surveillance program. Pew's national survey of 1,480 adults has found that the majority (70 percent), believe that the government uses data collected by the NSA for more than just the investigation of terrorism.[2] Findings in the Pew report also indicate that nearly half (47 percent) of Americans surveyed were concerned that government antiterrorism policies have begun restricting civil liberties.[3]

The privacy landscape continues to evolve with changes in technology, law, and in response to changing privacy concerns. What once was unthinkable, the ability of individuals, governments, and corporations to spy on an individual's activities both online and off, is now a reality. People make important decisions that impact their privacy on a daily basis, sometimes giving away privacy rights without realizing it. This can occur when doing such mundane things as automatically accepting the terms to download and use apps on smart phones without considering the terms of the agreement and browsing web pages or conducting transactions over the Internet without reading the privacy policies. In the United States the NSA surveillance program; the use of domestic surveillance drones[4] ; and other devices used by governments, businesses, and enterprising individuals to track, monitor, and record personal information means that even those with a careful eye on securing their information privacy will experience limits to their protection. The growing concern about the loss of information privacy and its impact on our daily lives, professional reputations, and the free exercise of our civil liberties highlights the importance of understanding what information privacy is and why we must fight to preserve it.

This first chapter will examine the origins of the right to privacy in the United States and the meaning of information privacy and related terms. Privacy rights will be placed in context to understand their origins in U.S. law and in other countries. A brief introduction and roadmap will then be provided to the remaining information privacy topics examined in this text.

ORIGINS OF PRIVACY RIGHTS

Peter P. Swire and Kenesa Ahmad explain that "the concept of information privacy as a social concept is rooted in some of the oldest texts and cultures." They cite references to privacy in the Bible, the Qur'an, Jewish law, and the laws of classical Greece.[5] There also existed early formal legal protections for privacy in laws dating as far back as 1361 in England. Laws in other parts of Europe dating to the 1700s have been enacted to address privacy issues. Privacy rights in the United States, like the country itself, are more recent in their creation.

U.S. Privacy Rights

Privacy and the U.S. Bill of Rights[6]

Though it is a common misconception, the term *privacy* does not appear in the *U.S. Constitution*. The *Bill of Rights* does contain language that reflects a focus on protecting certain aspects of privacy. Amendment I contains an implied privacy of religion or worship, providing that:

> Congress shall make no law respecting an establishment of religion, or prohibiting the free exercise thereof; or abridging the freedom of speech, or of the press; or the right of the people peaceably to assemble, and to petition the government for a redress of grievances.

Amendment IV reflects a concern for privacy of person, house, and belongings from searches and seizures. It provides:

> The right of the people to be secure in their persons, houses, papers, and effects, against unreasonable searches and seizures, shall not be violated, and

no warrants shall issue, but upon probable cause, supported by oath or affirmation, and particularly describing the place to be searched, and the persons or things to be seized.

Here, privacy is of a tangible nature.

Amendment V can also be seen as encompassing a privacy component, that of protection from intrusion. It holds in pertinent part that:

"No person shall . . . be deprived of life, liberty, or property, without due process of law; nor shall private property be taken for public use, without just compensation." [7]

Amendment XIV [8] extends this protection specifically to states by forbidding the creation or enforcement of state laws that abridge these rights.

The "Right to Privacy" Is Recognized

Nearly one hundred years after the *Bill of Rights* became law, Samuel Warren and Louis Brandeis (1890) published their seminal essay "The Right to Privacy" in the *Harvard Law Review*.[9] In it, they defined privacy as "the right to be let alone."[10] Warren and Brandeis wrote of the necessity of this protection because of the invasion of privacy by the press. While serving as Supreme Court Justice, Brandeis would affirm his definition of privacy in the context of government action in his dissent in *Olmstead v. United States*. In *Olmstead* Brandeis stated:

The makers of our Constitution . . . recognized the significance of man's spiritual nature, of his feelings, and of his intellect. . . . They sought to protect Americans in their beliefs, their thoughts, their emotions and their sensations. They conferred, as against the Government, the right to be let alone—the most comprehensive of rights, and the right most valued by civilized men. To protect that right, every unjustifiable intrusion by the Government upon the privacy of the individual, whatever the means employed, must be deemed a violation of the Fourth Amendment. And the use, as evidence in a criminal proceeding, of facts ascertained by such intrusion must be deemed a violation of the Fifth. [11]

Other cases have followed *Olmstead* that have also articulated privacy rights. Many definitions have been proposed for the meaning of privacy.

State Recognition of Privacy

Many state constitutions also provide privacy protections. Ten states specifically address the right of privacy in their constitutions. [12] Others provide statutory privacy protections for specific types of information, such as medical and financial records. These often add to the protections afforded by federal laws. Privacy protections may also be created through private contracts and privacy notices.

Invasion of privacy may be actionable under tort law. Tort law is state law and torts are civil wrongs that are recognized by law as a basis for lawsuits. These can include intrusion on seclusion, appropriation of one's name or likeness, public revelation of private facts, and false light in which the public disclosure of information is misleading. Lawsuits brought under state tort laws are different from those filed in response to large-scale personal data breaches, such as the Target breach of late 2013. The latter type are generally class-action suits for statutory damages, relying on provisions in federal laws that limit the circumstances in which certain types of personal data can be released. [13]

INFORMATION PRIVACY DEFINED

A study of privacy, a fundamental interest that is potentially so broad in scope, requires a working definition. Dr. Alan F. Westin defined *privacy* as "the claim of individuals, groups, or institutions to determine for themselves when, how, and to what extent information about them is communicated to others." [14] Westin's definition is particularly relevant for our examination as it provides us with a working definition of *information privacy*, which can be thought of as a subset of the more general right to privacy. [15] Westin published this definition during a time period (1961–1979) that he identifies as "the first Era of contemporary privacy development." This period is marked by a rise in awareness of the importance of information privacy and concerns about the impact of technology on privacy. Information privacy became "an explicit social, political, and legal issue." [16]

Westin's definition most closely matches the contemporary understanding of the meaning of *information privacy*. Indeed, Westin's definition has been cited by Kris Klein to define the meaning of *information privacy*, one of three recognized categories of privacy in Canada. [17] Similarly, Peter P. Swire and Kenesa Ahmad identify four classes of privacy (information privacy, bodily privacy, territorial privacy, and communications privacy). They identify information privacy as being "concerned with establishing rules that govern the collection and handling of personal information." [18] This would include personal information of all kinds including medical and financial information.

Personal Information

Certain terms are associated with information privacy and privacy law. It is important to have a basic understanding of the meaning of terms commonly used in discussions of information privacy, information privacy management, and in privacy laws. Introductory terms follow and will be placed in greater context and discussed with associated terms and ideas in later chapters.

Personal Data

The European Union, in Directive 95/46/EC also known as the Data Protection Directive, defines *personal data* as:

> Any information relating to an identified or identifiable natural person ("Data Subject"); an identifiable person is one who can be identified, directly or indirectly, in particular by reference to an identification number or to one or more factors specific to his physical, physiological, mental, economic, cultural or social identity. [19]

The Department of International Law of the Organization of American States (OAS), defines *personal data* as "all personal information of any kind . . . to any kind of data, whether or not private, that may affect rights if used by data processors." [20]

Data Protection

The OAS identifies *data protection* as an aspect of the right to privacy. It is the "right to privacy that people have against possible unauthorized use of personal information by a data processor . . . for the collection and misuse of personal data." [21]

Personally Identifiable Information

The term *personally identifiable information* (PII) [22] is used in privacy law in the United States to refer to personal data. What constitutes PII varies by country. Some countries are more encompassing in their definitions of PII than others.

Sensitive Personal Data

A subset of PII is *sensitive personal data*. In the United States it includes data that is specifically protected such as social security numbers, identifiable health records, and identifiable financial records.

Privacy Policy

A *privacy policy* is a document that instructs those within an organization [23] on data privacy as it applies to the collection and use of data within the organization. The audience for a privacy policy is employees of an organization. An organization may also use its privacy policy as a form of privacy notice when that policy is made available to those outside of the organization through actions such as placing the privacy policy on the organization's website.

Privacy Notice

A *privacy notice* is created by an organization and directed to the individuals from whom information will be collected and used by that organization. The privacy notice should describe how the organization collects, uses, and stores PII. Consumers rely on the information contained in privacy notices. Organizations are held to the terms of those notices by regulators. The terms contained in privacy notices are also generally binding on the individuals who receive notice.

THE DEVELOPMENT OF PRIVACY RIGHTS GLOBALLY

Privacy rights have a basis in human rights law. In 1948, the *Universal Declaration on Human Rights* was adopted by the General Assembly of the United Nations. The *Universal Declaration* addresses universal values including the right to privacy, which is specifically addressed in article 12:

> No one shall be subjected to arbitrary interference with his privacy, family, home or correspondence, nor to attacks upon his honour and reputation. Everyone has the right to the protection of the law against such interference or attacks. [24]

Earlier that same year, the *American Declaration of the Rights and Duties of Man* was adopted by the Ninth International Conference of American States[25] in Bogotá, Colombia. Article V of the *American Declaration* addresses the right of privacy. It provides that:

> Every person has the right to the protection of the law against abusive attacks upon his honor, his reputation, and his private and family life. [26]

The Council of Europe met in Rome in 1950 to invite council member states to sign the *European Convention for the Protection of Human Rights and Fundamental Freedoms.* The *Convention* followed in the vein of the *Universal Declaration* and provided privacy protection. Article 8 of the *Convention* provides:

1. Everyone has the right to respect for his private and family life, his home and his correspondence.
2. There shall be no interference by a public authority with the exercise of this right except such as is in accordance with the law and is necessary in a

democratic society in the interests of national security, public safety or the economic wellbeing of the country, for the prevention of disorder or crime, for the protection of health or morals, or for the protection of the rights and freedoms of others. [27]

Article 8 acknowledges the right to respect for privacy, but this is tempered with the acknowledgment that interference may occur if justified by national security or public interests.

In 1992, the United States ratified the *International Covenant on Civil and Political Rights*. The covenant is a legally binding international human rights agreement. Article 17 of this agreement specifically addresses privacy. It provides that:

1. No one shall be subjected to arbitrary or unlawful interference with his privacy, family, home or correspondence, nor to unlawful attacks on his honour and reputation.
2. Everyone has the right to the protection of the law against such interference or attacks. [28]

The declarations, convention, and covenant discussed above demonstrate the global concern for privacy as well as a significant level of international cooperation among countries seeking to safeguard privacy protections. It affirms the importance of privacy rights and protections for individuals across the globe.

TECHNOLOGY SPURS THE CREATION OF FAIR INFORMATION PRACTICE PRINCIPLES

In 1967, A. F. Westin defined *privacy* in relation to information in the technology age. The 1960s and 1970s were a time of technological advancements and increased concern about privacy. The growing ease with which data could be collected and transferred across international lines spurred economic growth but raised concerns about the handling and protection of private data. During this time many countries in Europe began implementing legislation to address these new privacy concerns. In the 1970s concerns about the adequacy of privacy protections led the Council of Europe to establish principles for the protection of personal data in the public and private sectors. [29] It was also in the 1970s that the Fair Information Practice Principles (FIPPs) took root in the United States. FIPPs have their origins in the U.S. Department of Health, Education and Welfare's 1973 report titled *Records, Computers and the Rights of Citizens*. FIPPs are at the core of the Privacy Act of 1974, [30] which serves to regulate the collection, use, and disclosure of personal information contained in the U.S. government system of records.

In 1981, the Organization for Economic Co-operation and Development (OECD) published "Guidelines Governing the Protection of Privacy and Transborder Data Flows of Personal Data." The OECD guidelines were developed to "prevent what are considered to be violations of fundamental human rights, such as the unlawful storage of personal data, the storage of inaccurate personal data, or the abuse or unauthorised disclosure of such data."[31] OECD members include most of the European countries, Australia, Canada, Chile, Israel, Japan, Republic of Korea, Mexico, New Zealand, Turkey, and the United States.[32]

More recently, in 2004, the Asia-Pacific Economic Cooperation (APEC) approved a privacy framework that sets out nine information privacy principles aligned with those of the OECD. The APEC is a multinational organization comprised of twenty-one members.[33] These countries have agreed to privacy principles to provide a flexible framework to govern the handling of private information. The principles they have approved align with those of the OECD and focus on preventing harm, limiting collection and use of personal information, providing notice, providing choice about collection where appropriate, maintaining the integrity of personal information and security safeguards, providing for access and correction, and ensuring for accountability when personal information is transferred.[34]

PROTECTING INFORMATION PRIVACY

Protecting information privacy is a professional imperative. Information privacy is necessary for intellectual freedom. If people are to feel free to exercise their right to receive information, they must feel secure that their preferences are not being monitored and will not be subject to negative consequences. The American Library Association (ALA) actively supports readers' privacy rights and has joined with the American Booksellers Association, the Association of American Publishers, and PEN American centers in a campaign for reader privacy. Together they have called on Congress to pass legislation that will restore privacy protections for library and bookstore patron/customer records that were removed by provisions in the PATRIOT Act.[35]

Protecting the privacy of library patrons is articulated in the Code of Ethics of the ALA.[36] Statement III of the code of ethics addresses the fundamental belief that library users have a right to privacy and confidentiality concerning the resources that they have "consulted, borrowed, acquired or transmitted."[37] The commitment of the ALA to the protection of patron privacy is evident in the multifold efforts they have made to bring attention to the problem of diminished patron privacy, to their professional stance on privacy, and to their educational efforts through mediums such as the ALA

Privacy Toolkit.[38] The professional position of the ALA concerning privacy is examined in greater depth in chapter 2.

U.S. FEDERAL AND STATE PRIVACY LAWS

Federal Privacy Laws

In the United States special privacy protections exist for specific types of sensitive data. Strict privacy and data protection laws exist for healthcare private information. The Health Insurance Portability and Accountability Act (HIPAA) is an example. HIPAA provides protections for personal information held by covered entities such as hospitals and their business associates. It permits these entities to disclose health information without permission only for certain specified purposes.

Private financial records are also specifically protected. The Gramm-Leach-Bliley Act of 1999 requires financial institutions to protect the consumer information they collect. Under this act, financial institutions are required to explain their information-sharing practices to customers.[39] More familiar to many readers is the Fair Credit Reporting Act (FCRA), which was enacted to ensure that consumer reporting agencies adopt reasonable procedures in credit reporting and provide consumers with the ability to access and correct the information about themselves contained within credit reports. This act also limits the use of consumer credit reports to certain "permissible purposes."[40]

Education records also enjoy special privacy protections in the United States. The Family Educational Rights and Privacy Act (FERPA) protects the privacy of student education records. It prevents schools from disclosing personally identifiable information derived from education records without the consent of the parent or eligible student unless specifically authorized under the act.[41] Special laws also apply to telecommunications and children's online privacy.

Those working in public libraries and schools are likely familiar with the Children's Internet Protection Act.[42] Many may not be aware of the Children's Online Privacy Protection Act (COPPA), an act that applies to the operators of commercial websites and online services that target their content to children under the age of thirteen. COPPA also applies to website owners who may not be targeting children directly, but who have actual knowledge that the information they are collecting is from minors under the age of thirteen. Under COPPA, a website operator targeting children, or with actual knowledge that the website information is being collected from children, is required to post a privacy policy on the website's homepage that provides notice to parents of the collection practices. COPPA requires that website operators attain verifiable parental consent before collecting information from minors. The Federal Trade Commission (FTC) is charged with enforcing COPPA.[43] Special privacy protections by sector under U.S. laws are discussed in depth in chapter 3.

State Privacy Laws

In addition to U.S. federal privacy laws, states have enacted their own privacy laws that can grant residents greater privacy protection. These laws are unique to each state and cover areas such as bank records, computer crime, credit information, employment records, medical records, school records, and tax records. Reading and understanding the privacy laws applicable in the state in which you reside and work is necessary to properly protect your own privacy rights and those of your patrons or clients.

Individual state consumer privacy information can often be found on or through the website of the attorney general for that state. Private compilation sources may also be available. At the time of this writing, a revised *Compilation of State and Federal Privacy Laws 2013* by Robert Ellis Smith is available.[44]

PRIVACY EDUCATION AND APPLICATION

Privacy Literacy

In addition to the special privacy protections that exist in the United States and in other countries, there are things individuals can actively do to protect their own information privacy. Part of our duty as information professionals is to educate others about information privacy. It is particularly important for those using online resources to understand what "web cookies"[45] are and how they work, the existence of persistent beacons, and how susceptible individuals are to hackers through the use of phishing. It is often said that a company's weakest area of defense is its employees. Proper education and regular training are needed to ensure the safety of information of individuals and entities. Information privacy literacy is examined further in chapter 4.

Information Privacy in Libraries

Many professionals and paraprofessionals employed in the library and information science field work with patrons who have more limited access to information and are often less knowledgeable about how to protect their privacy generally and especially in online environments. Chapter 5 examines information privacy in the library setting including issues such as observability; anonymity; and the need for staff to keep abreast of privacy issues, laws, and best practices. It also includes models that libraries can emulate, and it offers a new vision of the role of privacy professionals in libraries.

Understanding information privacy issues and the laws applicable to them provides the necessary foundation to begin developing information privacy policies. At the time of this writing, there is a shortage of trained information privacy professionals. The ability to demonstrate an understanding of privacy law; the role that information privacy policies play in libraries and other information organizations; and the knowledge of how to draft information privacy policies and procedures are useful skills for librarians and other information managers. The importance of information privacy policies, considerations for drafting policies, and the roles that managers of information privacy play in organizations is examined in chapter 6.

Applying Information Privacy Knowledge

Privacy policies anchor privacy programs that are crucial to ensuring the compliance of the organization and its employees with applicable privacy law. Understanding information privacy issues and the laws applicable to them provides the necessary foundation to begin developing information privacy policies not only for libraries but also for all organizations that collect, store, and utilize information about individuals. This subject and a brief overview of key elements involved in building an information privacy program are examined in chapter 6.

This text concludes with a brief look at global information privacy and fair information practices in chapter 7. Information can be transmitted on a global level in organizations that have offices in more than one country. Personally identifiable information regularly moves across national borders; information professionals need to be aware of privacy laws and practices that may impact their organizations and how to learn more about them.

NOTES

1. Pew Research Center, "Few See Adequate Limitations on NSA Surveillance Program," Washington, DC: Pew Research Center, July 26, 2013, www.people-press.org/files/legacy-pdf/7-26-2013%20NSA%20release.pdf. The Pew Research Center conducted this national study from July 17 to July 21, 2013, with 1,480 adult participants. Findings of this study show that participants were nearly split on their opinions of the government's collection of Internet and telephone data with 50 percent of participants approving of these actions and 44 percent disapproving.

2. Ibid., 4.

3. Ibid., 5.

4. Drones are unmanned aircraft, of varying sizes, equipped with surveillance equipment. The American Civil Liberties Union (ACLU) provides more information on drones and offers a useful list detailing the status of state legislation concerning drones in its December 2011 detailed report. ACLU, "Protecting Privacy from Aerial Surveillance: Recommendations for Government Use of Drone Aircraft," American Civil Liberties Union, last revised August 28,

2013,   www.aclu.org/blog/technology-and-liberty-national-security/what-fbi-needs-tell-americans-about-its-use-drones.

5. Peter P. Swire and Kenesa Ahmad, *Foundations of Information Privacy and Data Protection: A Survey of Global Concepts, Laws and Practices* (Portsmouth, NH: International Association of Privacy Professionals, 2012), 2.

6. The first ten amendments, known collectively as the *Bill of Rights*, became law in 1791. Several of these amendments address aspects of privacy and have been deemed to provide privacy rights including the First, Third, Fourth, Fifth, and Fourteenth amendments. The complete U.S. Constitution is available through the Legal Information Institute at www.law.cornell.edu/constitution.

7. The full text of Amendment V reads: "No person shall be held to answer for a capital, or otherwise infamous crime, unless on a presentment or indictment of a grand jury, except in cases arising in the land or naval forces, or in the militia, when in actual service in time of war or public danger; nor shall any person be subject for the same offense to be twice put in jeopardy of life or limb; nor shall be compelled in any criminal case to be a witness against himself, nor be deprived of life, liberty, or property, without due process of law; nor shall private property be taken for public use, without just compensation."

8. Amendment XIV, section 1 provides that "all persons born or naturalized in the United States, and subject to the jurisdiction thereof, are citizens of the United States and of the state wherein they reside. No state shall make or enforce any law which shall abridge the privileges or immunities of citizens of the United States; nor shall any state deprive any person of life, liberty, or property, without due process of law; nor deny to any person within its jurisdiction the equal protection of the laws."

9. Samuel Warren and Louis Brandeis, "The Right to Privacy," *Harvard Law Review* 4 (1890): 193–220, available online at http://groups.csail.mit.edu/mac/classes/6.805/articles/privacy/Privacy_brand_warr2.html.

10. Ibid., 193.

11. *Olmstead v. United States*, 277 U.S. 438, 478–79 (1928).

12. According to the National Conference of State Legislatures, the ten states that specifically recognize a right to privacy are: Alaska, Arizona, California, Florida, Hawaii, Illinois, Louisiana, Montana, South Carolina, and Washington. "Privacy Protections in State Constitutions," last updated December 11, 2013, www.ncsl.org/research/telecommunications-and-information-technology/privacy-protections-in-state-constitutions.aspx.

13. Lawrence T. Gresser and Karen Bromberg, "Litigation: Minimizing the Risk of Data Breach Class Actions from Target's Example," *Inside Counsel*, February 20, 2014, available online at www.insidecounsel.com/2014/02/20/litigation-minimizing-the-risk-of-data-breach-clas.

14. Alan F. Westin, *Privacy and Freedom* (New York: Atheneum, 1967), 7.

15. Westin uses his definition of *privacy* as the starting point for analyzing privacy in modern societies and defining information privacy in his article "Social and Political Dimensions of Privacy," *Journal of Social Issues* 59, no. 2 (2003): 431–53.

16. Ibid., 435.

17. Kris Klein, *Canadian Privacy: Data Protection Law and Policy for the Practitioner* (Portsmouth, NH: International Association of Privacy Professionals, 2012), 1. Klein identifies the three classes of privacy in Canadian law as information privacy, privacy of the person, and territorial privacy. Privacy of the person relates to "protects bodily integrity, and in particular the right not to have our bodies touched or explored to disclose objects or matters we wish to conceal." Territorial privacy relates to "placing limitations on the ability of an individual or organization to intrude into another individual's environment" (2).

18. Swire and Ahmad, *Foundations of Information Privacy and Data Protection*, 2. Swire and Ahmad identify bodily privacy as being "focused on a person's physical being and any invasion thereof." Territorial privacy relates to the placing of limits "on the ability to intrude into another individual's environment." They identify communications privacy as encompassing "protection of the means of correspondence." They do note that some categories interrelate as would be the case with communications privacy and information privacy.

19. Directive 95/46/EC of the European Parliament and of the Council of October 24, 1995, on the protection of individuals with regard to the processing of personal data and on the free movement of such data, Article 2, "Definitions," http://eur-lex.europa.eu (accessed February 10, 2014).

20. Department of International Law of the Organization of American States, "Data Protection," www.oas.org/dil/data_protection.htm (accessed August 26, 2013).

21. Ibid.

22. The Electronic Frontier Foundation offers an excellent discussion about how information that we believe might not be able to identify us actually can. Seth Schoen's 2009 article "What Information Is 'Personally Identifiable'?" explains how anonymous and demographic data may actually identify us. It is available at www.eff.org/deeplinks/2009/09/what-information-personally-identifiable.

23. The term *organization* is used generically here to refer to all forms of businesses including companies, corporations, foundations, and any other entities that collect data from individuals.

24. Office of the United Nations High Commissioner for Human Rights, *Universal Declaration of Human Rights* (December 1948), www.ohchr.org/EN/UDHR/Documents/UDHR_Translations/eng.pdf.

25. "American states" refers to the nations of the Americas that are members of the Organization of American States (OAS). As of 2014 all 35 countries of the Americas including the United States, Canada, and Cuba are members of the OAS (OAS 2014, http://www.oas.org/en/member_states/default.asp).

26. *American Declaration of the Rights and Duties of Man*, April 1948, Conference of American States, Article V, www.hrcr.org/docs/OAS_Declaration/oasrights5.html.

27. The Council of Europe, *European Convention on Human Rights*, http://conventions.coe.int/Treaty/en/Treaties/Html/005.htm.

28. Article 17 of the *International Covenant on Civil and Political Rights* (ICCPR), www.ohchr.org/en/professionalinterest/pages/ccpr.aspx. The ICCPR was ratified by the U.S. Senate in 1992.

29. Sian Rudgard, "Origins and Historical Context of Data Protection Law," in *Europe and Privacy: Law and Practice for Data Protection Professionals,* ed. Eduardo Ustaran (3–17) (Portsmouth, NH: International Association of Privacy Professionals, 2012), 6–7.

30. Privacy Act of 1974, 5 U.S.C. § 552a, as amended.

31. Organization for Economic Co-operation and Development, "Guidelines Governing the Protection of Privacy and Transborder Data Flows of Personal Data," preface, www.oecd.org/internet/ieconomy/oecdguidelinesontheprotectionofprivacyandtransborderflowsofpersonaldata.htm.

32. European OECD members: Austria, Belgium, Czech Republic, Denmark, Estonia, Finland, France, Germany, Greece, Hungary, Iceland, Ireland, Italy, Luxembourg, Netherlands, Norway, Poland, Portugal, Slovak Republic, Slovenia, Spain, Sweden, Switzerland, and United Kingdom. This information was taken directly from the OECD website at www.oecd.org/general/listofoecdmembercountries-ratificationoftheconventionontheoecd.htm.

33. Australia, Brunei Darussalam, Canada, Chile, China, Hong Kong, Indonesia, Japan, Republic of Korea, Malaysia, Mexico, New Zealand, New Guinea, Peru, Philippines, Russia, Singapore, Chinese Taipei, Thailand, United States, and Vietnam. "APEC Member Economies," *Asia-Pacific Economic Corporation* , www.apec.org/about-us/about-apec/member-economies.aspx (accessed April 12, 2014).

34. Asia Pacific Economic Cooperation (APEC) Privacy Framework, http://www.worldlii.org/int/other/PrivLRes/2005/4.html (accessed September 16, 2014).

35. The Campaign for Reader Privacy is an initiative of the American Booksellers Association, the ALA, the Association of American Publishers, and PEN American Center. The campaign has been working to restore reader privacy since 2004 and represents librarians, publishers, authors, and booksellers. More information about the campaign is available at www.readerprivacy.org. On July 18, 2013, the Campaign for Reader Privacy called on Congress to "pass legislation to restore privacy protections for bookstore and library records that were stripped by the PATRIOT Act as a first step toward reining in what the group calls

'runaway surveillance programs.'" This effort was documented in an ALA news press release available at www.ala.org/news/press-releases/2013/07/campaign-reader-privacy-renews-call-amend-patriot-act.

36. American Library Association, "Code of Ethics of the American Library Association," www.ala.org/advocacy/proethics/codeofethics/codeethics (accessed August 21, 2013).

37. Ibid., Statement III of the Code of Ethics of the ALA: "We protect each library user's right to privacy and confidentiality with respect to information sought or received and resources consulted, borrowed, acquired or transmitted."

38. The ALA Privacy Toolkit is an online resource that provides a forum for librarians and others to learn about privacy and includes links to the ALA's guidance on developing a privacy policy and information about conducting a privacy audit. It was updated in January 2014. "ALA Privacy Toolkit," www.ala.org/advocacy/privacyconfidentiality/toolkitsprivacy/privacy.

39. The Bureau of Consumer Protection provides information for institutions on how to comply with the Gramm-Leach-Bliley Act as well as helpful information for consumers at http://business.ftc.gov/privacy-and-security/gramm-leach-bliley-act.

40. The complete text of the Fair Credit Reporting Act (FCRA), 15 U.S.C. § 1681 et seq., is available at www.ftc.gov/os/statutes/031224fcra.pdf.

41. A more detailed explanation of the FERPA can be found on the U.S. Department of Education's website at www2.ed.gov/policy/gen/guid/fpco/ferpa/students.html.

42. The Children's Internet Protection Act (CIPA) was enacted by Congress in 2000, and its constitutionality was affirmed by the U.S. Supreme Court on June 23, 2003. CIPA was enacted to protect children from harmful or obscene content on the Internet. It requires libraries that receive discounts on Internet access or internal connections through the E-rate program to certify that they have an Internet safety policy that includes technology protection measures that block or filter Internet access to harmful, obscene, or pornographic images on the computers accessible to minors.

43. In July 2013, the Federal Trade Commission published its revised guide for complying with COPPA. The guide, which offers information for businesses and parents, is available at www.business.ftc.gov/documents/Complying-with-COPPA-Frequently-Asked-Questions.

44. Robert Ellis Smith (2013), *Compilation of State and Federal Privacy Laws 2013*, Providence, RI: Privacy Journal. This source includes a 2014 supplement and an appendix of Canadian federal and provincial laws.

45. Web cookies are small text files that are placed by websites onto our computers to allow web servers to store information there.

BIBLIOGRAPHY

ACLU. "Protecting Privacy from Aerial Surveillance: Recommendations for Government Use of Drone Aircraft." Last revised August 28, 2013. www.aclu.org/blog/technology-and-liberty-national-security/what-fbi-needs-tell-americans-about-its-use-drones.

Klein, Kris. *Canadian Privacy: Data Protection Law and Policy for the Practitioner*. Portsmouth, NH: International Association of Privacy Professionals, 2012.

Pew Research Center. "Few See Adequate Limitations on NSA Surveillance Program." Washington, DC: Pew Research Center, July 26, 2013. www.people-press.org/files/legacy-pdf/7-26-2013%20NSA%20release.pdf.

Rudgard, Sian. "Origins and Historical Context of Data Protection Law." In *Europe and Privacy: Law and Practice for Data Protection Professionals*, edited by Eduardo Ustaran (3–17). Portsmouth, NH: International Association of Privacy Professionals, 2012.

Schoen, Seth. "What Information Is 'Personally Identifiable'?" Electronic Frontier Foundation, September 11, 2009. www.eff.org/deeplinks/2009/09/what-information-personally-identifiable.

Smith, Robert E. *Compilation of State and Federal Privacy Laws 2013*. Providence, RI: Privacy Journal, 2013.

Stanley, Jay, and Catherine Crump. "Protecting Privacy from Aerial Surveillance: Recommendations for Government Use of Drone Aircraft." American Civil Liberties Union, December 2011. www.aclu.org/files/assets/protectingprivacyfromaerialsurveillance.pdf.

Swire, Peter P., and Kenesa Ahmad. *Foundations of Information Privacy and Data Protection: A Survey of Global Concepts, Laws and Practices.* Portsmouth, NH: International Association of Privacy Professionals, 2012.

Warren, Samuel, and Louis Brandeis. "The Right to Privacy." *Harvard Law Review* 4 (1890): 193–220. Available online at http://groups.csail.mit.edu/mac/classes/6.805/articles/privacy/Privacy_brand_warr2.html.

Westin, Alan F. *Privacy and Freedom.* New York: Athenum, 1967.

———. "Social and Political Dimensions of Privacy." *Journal of Social Issues* 59, no. 2 (2003): 431–53.

Chapter Two

Protecting Information Privacy

A Professional Imperative

Protecting information privacy is a professional imperative for all information professionals. In the United States, Canada, the European Union, and in many other parts of the world individuals enjoy privacy rights. They have an expectation that their privacy rights will be observed when they seek information in libraries and other information environments and when they provide information in educational, medical, and financial settings. If people do not feel free to seek, create, and share information and ideas freely and without scrutiny or other negative effects, many will not. Even what may be perceived as minor intrusions on privacy can impede the free flow of ideas hindering information seeking, critical thinking, and the development of new ideas and opinions based on the receipt and evaluation of new information. Contravening privacy rights thus lead to a stunting of creativity and innovation that impacts all of us.

PROTECTING PRIVACY IN INFORMATION ENVIRONMENTS

Growing concerns about information privacy point to gaps in the protection of information. Today, private- and public-sector organizations have an increased focus on data mining[1] and the ways in which information can be used to increase profits, predict trends, and market products and services. At the same time, information privacy is coming under greater pressure as the desire of individuals to keep their information and interests private competes with the interests of business and government entities to track, monitor, and harness information. It is important to remember that the protection of privacy rights should be a consideration for all information professionals as they perform their daily job duties, plan for future projects and actions, address novel issues, and respond to requests for information from internal and external sources.

In the United States, laws specifically address the privacy protection of certain information generated about individuals such as medical records, education records, and financial records. Efforts are made to protect information that individuals generate but choose to keep private and about which they have an expectation of privacy such as e-mail correspondence and telephone conversations. Unless publicly shared or subject to a wiretap or other clandestine investigation, most individuals expect that information shared through these channels of communications will remain relatively private. Although a party to the e-mail or telephone conversation might share this information, it is generally not expected to be the subject of governmental surveillance or broad public exposure.

As information professionals, each of us must make information privacy a priority. We must consider our own actions and those that might occur in our work environments. We must ask how these actions might affect the privacy rights of people with whom we do business, the patrons using our libraries, and the individuals who have entrusted their information to us even if they have done so unknowingly. An overview of laws and case law interpretations addressing the right to receive information and the privacy afforded this right generally and in certain information environments is helpful to ground this discussion.

PRIVACY AND THE RIGHT TO RECEIVE INFORMATION

The right to receive information is of paramount importance in information environments such as libraries. The right to receive information is protected on many different levels. Guiding countries at the international level, the United Nations addresses freedom of opinion and expression, including the right to receive information without interference in Article 19 of the *Universal Declaration of Human Rights*.[2] This right is echoed in the *International Covenant on Civil and Political Rights*,[3] to which many countries, including the United States and Canada, are parties.

In *Martin v. Struthers* (1943)[4] the U.S. Supreme Court acknowledged the right to receive information as inextricably tied to the First Amendment right of freedom of speech. In *Martin*, the right of an individual to knock door-to-door and distribute religious leaflets was considered, the U.S. Supreme Court weighed in on the right of freedom of speech. Justice Black, delivering the opinion of the Court, explained that freedom of speech "embraces the right to distribute literature (citation omitted) and necessarily protects the right to receive it."[5]

Building on the connection between freedom of speech and the right to receive information as articulated in *Martin*, the U.S. Supreme Court in *Griswold v. Connecticut* (1965)[6] went further in explaining the relationship. In *Griswold*, defendants appealed a conviction under a Connecticut statute that made it a criminal offense to use contraceptives. Defendants were convicted as accessories for providing information and instruction to married individuals about the means of preventing pregnancy. In reversing the conviction the Supreme Court of the United States found that the statute was an unconstitutional invasion of the privacy of married individuals.[7] More importantly, for the purposes of our discussion, it identified the right to receive information as one of the "peripheral rights" that are associated with the freedom of speech and press.[8] The Court explained that "specific guarantees in the Bill of Rights have penumbras, formed by emanations from those guarantees that help give them life and substance (citation omitted). Various guarantees create zones of privacy."[9]

Privacy was considered again in the context of the right to receive information in *Stanley v. Georgia* (1969).[10] In *Stanley*, the Court reviewed the conviction of the appellant for knowingly possessing obscene material in violation of a Georgia law. The obscene material was discovered in the appellant's home during the execution of a search warrant for evidence on an unrelated matter. In reversing the conviction and remanding the case, the U.S. Supreme Court commented on the right to receive information, even information deemed obscene, finding that "mere private possession of obscene matter cannot constitutionally be made a crime."[11] Delivering its opinion through Justice Marshall, the Court made clear that the constitutional right to receive information and ideas[12] is not based on the perceived value of the information and ideas. The court referenced *Winters v. New York*,[13] declaring that:

> this right to receive information and ideas, regardless of their social worth . . . is fundamental to our free society. Moreover, in the context of this case—a prosecution for mere possession of printed or filmed matter in the privacy of a person's own home—that right takes on an added dimension. For also fundamental is the right to be free, except in very limited circumstances, from unwanted governmental intrusions into one's privacy.[14]

Furthering its stance on the importance of the right to receive information free from intrusion and scrutiny, the *Stanley* court cited Justice Brandeis's famous dissent in *Olmstead*, declaring:

> The makers of our Constitution undertook to secure conditions favorable to the pursuit of happiness. They recognized the significance of man's spiritual na-

ture, of his feelings and of his intellect. . . . They sought to protect Americans in their beliefs, their thoughts, their emotions and their sensations. They conferred, as against the Government, the right to be let alone—the most comprehensive of rights and the right most valued by civilized man. [15]

These early cases paved the way for our understanding of the relationship of the right to receive information to freedom of speech and press rights. They highlight the value the Supreme Court of the United States has placed on privacy particularly as it relates to receiving information and ideas in the home and protecting against government intrusion.

The Right to Receive Information in Libraries

Do the same protections concerning the right to receive information extend to information environments such as libraries? An overview of case law addressing this question can help librarians and other information professionals understand the ethical stances and core value statements supporting information privacy of associations such as ALA, the Society of American Archivists, the International Medical Informatics Association, and others.

The right to receive information in a public school library setting was affirmed by the U.S. Supreme Court in *Board of Education v. Pico* (1982). [16] *Pico* involved a challenge by students to a school board order to remove books from the district high school and junior high that it deemed objectionable. The U.S. Supreme Court, in a plurality opinion, stated that "the right to receive ideas is a necessary predicate to the *recipient's* meaningful exercise of his own rights of speech, press, and political freedom." [17] The Court, in affirming the right to receive information, did place some limits on that right in a public school environment if materials are "educationally unsuitable" or "pervasively vulgar." [18]

The rights of minors to receive information in libraries may be further restricted if the information is obscene, harmful to minors, or child pornography. Obscene speech is not protected by the First Amendment, and public libraries participating in certain federal funding programs or state funding may be subject to the Children's Internet Protection Act and state harmful-to-minors laws, which are currently in effect in twenty-four states. [19]

INTELLECTUAL PRIVACY

The legal reasons to protect information privacy have been discussed, but other equally compelling reasons exist. By protecting information privacy, information professionals are also guarding the freedom of individuals to cultivate interests, learn about themselves, and develop their own likes and dislikes, and beliefs freely. Protecting information privacy allows individuals to feel free to sample the marketplace of ideas without fear of interference or scrutiny, which could inhibit curiosity. This type of freedom of the mind has been defined by Neil M. Richards as intellectual privacy. [20]

This freedom of the mind, or intellectual privacy, is needed to facilitate the development of critical reasoning and information literacy. Children, young adults, and adults need the security of knowing that their private information is kept private and that they can rely on the confidentiality of information professionals as they explore their information interests and needs. It is important for everyone learning how to evaluate information sources and to think critically about these sources that they feel free to question information without fear of negative consequences. This exploration is part of information literacy and is crucial to the development of critical reasoning abilities that are needed to thrive in today's global information society.

Not knowing if their private information will be protected can deter individuals from seeking information, from exchanging it with others, and ultimately from producing it. The fear of scrutiny and exposure can inhibit the search process, limit the avenues that individuals feel free to explore, and discourage free investigation. This is detrimental not just to individuals but also to society as a whole as it has the potential to limit new ideas and actions. Fewer individuals will be willing to explore new ideas if there may be unknown consequences for doing so.

After all, who among us would really want every Internet search we performed revealed publicly, not just by agents of the government, but also by potential employers? Even if the information sought is not lascivious or illegal, it may not present us in the best light or it might mix our public and private faces. We may not want work colleagues to know about certain aspects of our personal lives. What about searches for health information, marital counseling, financial counseling? While these types of information searches may not be the focus of current information gathering, large-scale unchecked information gathering runs the risk of exposing this type of information and more.

We need protection of our private information for unfettered intellectual exploration and to develop the critical thinking skills needed for today's jobs. Recent business articles highlight the problem of a skills gap between job applicants and the jobs available. [21] One skill that is often mentioned is critical thinking. When the ability to search, question, and grow without being scrutinized is removed, critical thinking skills become even more elusive.

In a time when search engines are trying to anticipate our needs and steer us to information effortlessly, it is crucial that there remains a level of information privacy to allow for intellectual exploration, to stimulate the mind, to test our own likes and dislikes, and to understand—through exposure to a wide range of information—what sources we deem valuable and how to determine and select the useful and relevant from the many available. The freedom of information privacy and the ability to determine our own information interests free from scrutiny or proscription is necessary to develop as individuals and hone our critical thinking and reasoning skills to be able to compete locally and globally. The protection of information privacy in libraries allows them to remain places of intellectual freedom and exploration. If we choose not to protect information privacy in these environments we risk turning our libraries into outposts of business and government information gathering.

READER PRIVACY

The ALA, through its Office of Intellectual Freedom, should be commended for its continuing fight for reader privacy and the overall privacy of library users. Through these efforts, the focus remains on privacy rather than increasing organizations' and government access to reader records in libraries. The efforts of the ALA, along with state laws protecting library record privacy and confidentiality, help to safeguard patron reader records.[22] Reader privacy may still be subject to properly issued government search warrants, including National Security Letters authorized under the expanded powers afforded by the USA PATRIOT Act[23] and court orders, but the response to these information requests are matters to be discussed with the library's legal advisors.

Users do not enjoy the same protection concerning their book purchasing records from bookstores. The records of customers' video rentals may be protected under the Video Privacy Protection Act,[24] which prevents disclosure of records of video rentals and similar audiovisual materials, but in general the same protections are not available to customers' book-purchasing records. So far, only two states have passed specific protections for book-purchase records. In 2009 both Rhode Island and Michigan enacted laws to protect records of book purchases.[25]

Even given the lack of specific state protections, some bookstores have taken a stand for reader privacy, notably the Tattered Cover Bookstore in Denver, Colorado. In *Tattered Cover, Inc. v. City of Thornton* (2002)[26] a bookstore owner refused a government request for a customer's book purchasing records. In April 2000, police officers armed with a warrant arrived at the Tattered Cover demanding the book purchasing records of a customer it suspected of illegal drug making. The owner of the bookstore refused, asserting the constitutional rights of the bookseller and those of the customers under the First Amendment and Article 2, Section 10 of the Colorado Constitution. The case made its way to the Supreme Court of Colorado, which recognized that "both the First Amendment of the United States Constitution and Article II, Section 10 of the Colorado Constitution protect an individual's fundamental right to purchase books anonymously, free from government interference."[27] While the Tattered Cover is not alone in protecting the privacy rights of customers, the lack of widespread specific state protections means that the privacy of book purchasers may not be as secure as those of library users. In most states, decisions about the value of reader privacy are left to the bookstore.

The American Civil Liberties Union of Northern California recently released a publication that examines issues of reader privacy when using digital books. In it, author Nicole A. Ozer points out that digital book providers can gather more information about readers' habits from these books than their paper counterparts. Information can be gathered about the time spent browsing and reading, along with details that identify the reader's Internet protocol (IP) address among other things.[28] The information gathered may be used for business purposes including data mining and may be vulnerable to demands for access by agents of the government. Ozer explains that the fear that this type of information gathering and retention may be abused could have a chilling effect on people's desire to use such sites.[29] Given the vulnerability of reader privacy concerning book purchase records and online digital services, the need for information professionals in libraries and other information environments to protect reader privacy is even more important.

Concern for reader privacy and information privacy in general should not be undervalued. The information privacy rights that we protect professionally are also our own and those of our families and friends. What may seem to be innocuous information gathering today could become something different in the future. It remains uncertain what collectors of our private information are currently using it for and what they will do with it in the future. It is a fallacy to assume that the protection of information privacy is someone else's responsibility. It is reckless to assume that all businesses, service providers, and agents of the government are aware of and abiding by the laws designed to protect information privacy. News reports, case law, and information from federal regulating agencies tell us otherwise. If we fail to protect information privacy, we are essentially bathing with the curtains open.

PROFESSIONAL IMPORTANCE OF PROTECTING INFORMATION PRIVACY

Information privacy must be a concern for all who work in information professions. Awareness of laws affecting the gathering, use, storage, and security of personally identifiable information is needed to perform job duties and remain compliant with legal requirements and industry standards. Technology continues to bring about rapid changes in the information landscape and information professionals must remain vigilant about educating themselves to keep up with these changes. Ethical guidelines from professional associations serve to guide professionals, informing members of the profession, and other interested parties about the principles to which a profession is committed. A sampling of ethical statements and core values from several associations for information professionals follows. Each recognizes the importance of safeguarding information privacy.

Library Associations

The ALA has been vocal in its support for privacy of its patrons and their information. The Code of Ethics of the ALA[30] (COE) addresses privacy specifically. Statement III of the COE states that librarians "protect each library user's right to privacy and confidentiality with respect to information sought or received and resources consulted, borrowed, acquired or transmitted."

The ALA's support of information privacy is also evident in the resources it has created for librarians and others. The ALA Intellectual Freedom Manual addresses privacy and the ALA provides an online privacy toolkit. The ALA website prominently posts this unequivocal message: "Privacy is essential to the exercise of free speech, free thought, and free association" at the beginning of the "Interpretation of the Library Bill of Rights"[31] on the topic of privacy.

The Canadian Library Association (CLA) also has recognized the importance of information privacy and addresses it specifically in their position statement on access to information and communication technology. The CLA's position statement includes an assertion that the personal information that is available on information and communication technology (ICT) networks should be protected by legislation. Also contained in the statement is the guidance that there should be a written statement outlining the purpose for the collection of any personal data, that the collection should be limited to outlined purposes, and that personal data should only be collected, used, and shared with the consent of the individual. The CLA's position statement makes it clear that personal data should not be traded or sold without express written permission of the individual and that information about privacy policies should be readily accessible and provide for an "opt-in" option for any changes that are made to these policies.[32] The "opt-in" provision stands in contrast to the "opt-out" option that is prevalent in the United States. The CLA's position statement supports the rights of individuals to examine their own personal information and to correct mistakes without charge.

The International Federation of Library Associations and Institutions (IFLA), a leading advisory force in the library and information professions, strongly supports information privacy. Section 3 of the IFLA Code of Ethics for Librarians and other Information Workers addresses privacy. The IFLA Code of Ethics states that "librarians and other information workers respect personal privacy, and the protection of personal data, necessarily shared between individuals and institutions." It goes on to find confidential the relationship between libraries and users.[33] In short, the support for information privacy by library and information professionals is both widespread and multinational.

Archivists Associations

Archivists also recognize the importance of information privacy and the need to respect the legal and cultural importance of privacy. The Society of American Archivists's (SAA) Core Values focus in part on access and use that is consistent with business, institutional, or personal privacy. The SAA Code of Ethics recognizes the need for and seeks to establish procedures for maintaining privacy and confidentiality of donors, individuals, groups, and institutions whose public and private lives are recorded in the holdings, as well as the privacy of users.[34] Similarly, the Association of Canadian Archivists' Code of Ethics contains several statements about privacy, noting the need to give attention to and protect personal privacy when selecting, preserving, and making materials available for use.[35] One of the ten points of the Code of Ethics of the International Council on Archives (ICA) focuses on respect for corporate privacy, personal privacy, and national security.[36] Archivists should respect the personal privacy of individuals who created records or were the subjects of records.[37]

Medical Informatics and Health Information Management Associations

The International Medical Informatics Association's Code of Ethics for Health Information Professionals has as its first general principle of information ethics a statement addressing information privacy disposition that acknowledges the fundamental right to privacy that individuals have and their right "to control over the collection, storage, access, use, communication, manipulation and disposition of data about themselves."[38] The code explains that any infringement on an individual's privacy rights and the right to control data about themselves "may only occur in the least intrusive fashion and with a minimum of interference" to the rights of that person. This code goes on to require that such infringement be timely and appropriately justified to the individual.[39]

Similarly, the Code of Ethics of the American Health Information Management Association (AHIMA) addresses both privacy and security of health information throughout the code. The second paragraph acknowledges the privacy and security concerns of healthcare consumers. In the accompanying principles and guidelines, AHIMA advises health information management professionals to "advocate, uphold, and defend the individual's right to privacy and the doctrine of confidentiality in the use and disclosure of information." Associations focused on healthcare information management provide some of the strongest ethical statements about the use of personal information and the need to respect and uphold privacy.

ARMA International (ARMA), formerly the Association of Records Managers and Administrators, counts among its members information managers, archivists, corporate librarians, and recently certified information governance professionals.[40] ARMA's Code of Ethics for Information Governance Professionals (IGP) is perhaps the most encompassing of those examined for this chapter. IGPs are charged not only with protecting personal property but also with maintaining the confidentiality of proprietary information and complying with law. An ethical and moral duty is also imposed on IGPs for the use of information.

The examples above make clear that professional information associations have considered many of the information privacy issues facing individuals today and support privacy as an ethical stance that is shared among those working in the professions and members of these organizations. This is a prudent decision as it places them in agreement with current laws and policies and enhances the credibility of their professions. This can be a boon to the professions socially and economically.

Understanding and complying with information privacy laws is part of the professional duties of librarians and other information professionals. As we have seen, the duty to protect information privacy is present in ethical statements of core values of professional organizations devoted to information management, information science, librarianship, and preservation. Just as doctors and lawyers have professional codes of conduct that guide their professional behavior, so too do informational professionals. Like these other professionals, we must take seriously our duties and ensure that we each make protecting information privacy a professional priority. Our ethical codes provide us with the professional principles to uphold. Key among them is the protection of information privacy.

CONCLUSION

Every day, librarians and other information professionals are confronted with privacy issues as they provide library services to patrons and manage information across the globe. They must make decisions about how they will protect the privacy of individuals as well as other rights that are collectively identified as intellectual freedom rights. In the United States the First,

Fourth, and Fourteenth Amendments to the U.S. Constitution form the basis of our understanding of information privacy protection in conjunction with specialized federal laws and privacy laws enacted by states. Overlaying these protections, at the international level, are treaties and covenants to which the United States is a party. Together they provide a foundation to inform and guide information professionals as they seek to safeguard the information privacy rights of individuals.

The privacy of personal information is suffering encroachments through investigations authorized under the USA PATRIOT Act, government surveillance, and data mining. In light of this, it is crucially important that there remain avenues for protected exploration and intellectual freedom. Information privacy is imperative for intellectual freedom. Individuals need venues where they can explore interests and information free from scrutiny to develop critical thinking skills, form opinions, and determine beliefs. If we do not protect information privacy, it will be eroded through current technology practices, default sharing, and the actions of businesses and agents of the government, to the point that any expectation of privacy is lost.

NOTES

1. Data mining involves the analyzing of data for patterns or relationships. It is often employed by businesses to discover relationships that can increase revenue. Data-mining software may be used to analyze information in different ways to reveal relationships that may be used to increase profits through a number of different means including the sale of the information. A recent example of data mining for revenue enhancement is the proposed use of Google+ users' faces and reviews to market products to others. CNN provides an overview of the Google advertising, which is slated to go into effect November 11, 2013. See the October 11, 2013, article "Why Your Face Might Appear in Google Ads, and How to Stop It" by Heather Kelly at www.cnn.com/2013/10/11/tech/social-media/google-plus-ads-profiles (accessed October 11, 2013).

2. Article 19 of the Universal Declaration of Human Rights provides: "Everyone has the right to freedom of opinion and expression; this right includes freedom to hold opinions without interference and to seek, receive and impart information and ideas through any media and regardless of frontiers." Available on the United Nations website at www.un.org/en/documents/udhr/index.shtml#a19 (accessed October 14, 2013).

3. The International Covenant on Civil and Political Rights, Article 19, provides the following:

1. Everyone shall have the right to hold opinions without interference.
2. Everyone shall have the right to freedom of expression; this right shall include freedom to seek, receive and impart information and ideas of all kinds, regardless of frontiers, either orally, in writing or in print, in the form of art, or through any other media of his choice.
3. The exercise of the rights provided for in paragraph 2 of this article carries with it special duties and responsibilities. It may therefore be subject to certain restrictions, but these shall only be such as are provided by law and are necessary (a) for respect of the rights or reputations of others, or (b) for the protection of national security or of public order (order public), or of public health or morals." United Nations, Human Rights, Office of the High Commissioner for Human Rights, International Covenant on

Civil and Political Rights available at www.ohchr.org/en/professionalinterest/pages/ccpr.aspx, accessed October 14, 2013.

4. *Martin v. Struthers*, 319 U.S. 141 (1943).

5. Ibid. at 143.

6. *Griswold v. Connecticut*, 381 U.S. 479 (1965).

7. Ibid. at 486.

8. Ibid. at 482-483.

9. Ibid. at 484.

10. *Stanley v. Georgia*, 394 U.S. 557 (1969).

11. Ibid. at 559.

12. The Court cited *Martin v. City of Struthers*, 319 U.S. 141, 143 (1943), *Griswold v. Connecticut*, 381 U.S. 479 (1965), and Lamont v. Postmaster General, 381 U.S. 301 (1965), in support of the Constitutional right to receive information and ideas.

13. *Winters v. New York*, 333 U.S. 507, 510 (1948).

14. *Stanley v. Georgia* at 564.

15. *Stanley v. Georgia* at 564, citing *Olmstead v. United States*, 277 U.S. 438, 478 (1928) (J. Brandeis, dissenting).

16. *Board of Education v. Pico*, 457 U.S. 855 (1982).

17. Ibid. at 867.

18. Ibid. at 890.

19. "Children and the Internet Laws Relating to Filtering, Blocking and Usage Policies in Schools and Libraries," National Conference of State Legislators, last modified September 13, 2013, www.ncsl.org/issues-research/telecom/state-internet-filtering-laws.aspx.

20. In 2008, Neil M. Richards defined the term *intellectual privacy* as referring to "the protection of records of our intellectual activities." He identified this protection as "essential" to free thought and expression. Neil M. Richards, "Intellectual Privacy," *Texas Law Review* 87, no. 2 (2008): 387.

21. See Jeff Selingo, "Skills Gap? Employers and Colleges Point Fingers at Each Other," *The Chronicle of Higher Education*, September 12, 2012, http://chronicle.com/blogs/next/2012/09/12/skills-gap-employers-and-colleges-point-fingers-at-each-other; Allen Wastler, "Job Skills Gap: The Basics Become a Problem," *CNBC.com*, September 2, 2013, www.cnbc.com/id/101012437; and David Smith, "How Employers Can Help Solve the Skills Gap," *Harvard Business Review*, February 9, 2012, http://blogs.hbr.org/2012/02/how-employers-can-help-solve-t.

22. The ALA, through the Office of Intellectual Freedom, provides links to forty-eight state laws and opinions of two attorneys general that address the privacy and confidentiality of library records across the United States, available at www.ala.org/offices/oif/ifgroups/stateifc-chairs/stateifcinaction/stateprivacy (accessed October 16, 2013). Though the states and district do not provide identical protections, these laws and opinions serve to guide information professionals working in libraries in those states as they seek to protect patron privacy rights.

23. The USA PATRIOT Act allows federal investigators broader powers to investigate domestic terrorism. The full text of the USA PATRIOT Act is available at www.gpo.gov/fdsys/pkg/PLAW-107publ56/pdf/PLAW-107publ56.pdf.

24. The full text of the Video Privacy Protection Act, 18 U.S.C. 2710—Wrongful Disclosure of Video Tape Rental or Sale Records, is available through the U.S. Government Printing Office's Federal Digital System, FDsys, at www.gpo.gov/fdsys/granule/USCODE-2011-title18/USCODE-2011-title18-partI-chap121-sec2710/content-detail.html.

25. Rhode Island. Gen. Laws §11-18-32 (2009); Mich. Comp. Laws Ann. § 445.1712 (2009), as noted on page 3 and endnote 9. Nicole A. Ozer, "Digital Books: A New Chapter for Reader Privacy," American Civil Rights Union of Northern California, March 2010, www.aclunc.org/sites/default/files/asset_upload_file295_9047.pdf.

26. *Tattered Cover, Inc. v. City of Thornton* 44 P.3d 1044 (Colo. 2002).

27. Ibid. at 1047.

28. Ozer, "Digital Books," 4.

29. Ibid., 5.

30. The full text of the ALA COE is available at www.ala.org/advocacy/proethics/code-ofethics/codeethics. The COE includes eight statements addressing service, intellectual freedom and censorship, privacy and confidentiality, intellectual property, treatment of coworkers and colleagues, private interests versus those of the user, personal convictions, and striving for excellence through knowledge and professional development.

31. "Privacy," American Library Association, July 7, 2006, www.ala.org/advocacy/intfreedom/librarybill/interpretations/privacy (accessed September 9, 2013). Document ID: 5c653c23-920b-b254-d94c-6dcf4ccd86c6.

32. Canadian Library Association Position Statement on Access to Information and Communication Technology (ICT) available at www.cla.ca/AM/Template.cfm? Section=Position_Statements&Template=/CM/ContentDisplay.cfm&ContentID=3046.

33. IFLA Code of Ethics for Librarians and Other Information Workers is available at www.ifla.org/news/ifla-code-of-ethics-for-librarians-and-other-information-workers-full-version#privacy (accessed October 17, 2013).

34. The Society of American Archivists Statements of Core Values and Code of Ethics is available at www2.archivists.org/statements/saa-core-values-statement-and-code-of-ethics (accessed September 21, 2013).

35. Association of Canadian Archivists, Code of Ethics, available at http://archivists.ca/content/code-ethics (accessed October 17, 2013).

36. International Council of Archives, Code of Ethics, available at www.ica.org/5555/reference-documents/ica-code-of-ethics.html (accessed October 17, 2013).

37. International Council of Archives, Code of Ethics, code 7.

38. International Medical Informatics Association, Code of Ethics for Health Information Professionals, available at www.imia-medinfo.org/new2/pubdocs/Ethics_Eng.pdf (accessed October 17, 2013).

39. International Medical Informatics Association, Code of Ethics, principles 6 and 7.

40. ARMA recently launched a new certification for information governance professionals.

BIBLIOGRAPHY

"Children and the Internet Laws Relating to Filtering, Blocking and Usage Policies in Schools and Libraries." *National Conference of State Legislators*. Last modified September 13, 2013. www.ncsl.org/issues-research/telecom/state-internet-filtering-laws.aspx.

Office of Intellectual Freedom, comp. *Intellectual Freedom Manual*. 8th edition. Chicago: American Library Association, 2010.

Ozer, Nicole A. "Digital Books: A New Chapter for Reader Privacy." *American Civil Rights Union of Northern California*, March 2010. www.aclunc.org/sites/default/files/asset_upload_file295_9047.pdf.

Richards, Neil M. "Intellectual Privacy." *Texas Law Review* 87, no. 2 (2008): 387–445.

Schauer, Frederick. "Fear, Risk and the First Amendment: Unraveling the 'Chilling Effect.'" B. U. L. Review 58 (1978): 685–732.

Chapter Three

Major U.S. Privacy Protections

Laws, Regulators, and Approaches to Enforcement

INTRODUCTION

Understanding information privacy requires an awareness of the risks involved in the dissemination of personally identifiable information, referred to as personal information or personal data,[1] and of the laws and regulators that govern personal data dissemination. Ensuring data privacy includes understanding and applying applicable privacy laws through the creation of policies, procedures, and security measures, as well as privacy training to ensure that personal data is handled appropriately. On a practical level, data security is addressed by information systems security personnel who manage the physical and technical aspects of security. However, to ensure information privacy, the physical measures must work in conjunction with legal measures, policies, and programs also designed to safeguard data privacy. Even the best technical security is vulnerable to the actions of employees who may inadvertently or intentionally bypass security measures, fail to adhere to privacy and security standards, and expose data through unsafe practices.

Knowing what laws govern the handling of personal data in various information settings and understanding the role of federal regulating agencies can help information professionals ensure that personal data is handled in a legal and prudent manner. Major U.S. privacy laws and regulators are the focus of this chapter, which will provide information professionals with an introduction to this aspect of information privacy.

Unlike the European Union's Data Protection Directive of 1995,[2] discussed in chapter 1, the United States does not have a comprehensive data privacy law. This has recently become a point of concern for many as news reports publicize allegations that the National Security Agency (NSA) has undertaken extensive data surveillance activities with the assistance of companies in private industry to intercept data being transferred domestically and abroad.[3] Concern about this widespread surveillance is affecting international relations[4] with officials from European countries who have expressed concerns about the privacy of their citizens.[5]

The United States has taken a sectoral approach to protecting information privacy rights. This approach utilizes a combination of legislation, regulation, and self-regulation. This can be thought of as a three-layer system. The top layer is legislation. Legislation is the "preparation and enactment of laws."[6] In some cases regulations are needed to specify how to comply with laws. Certain federal agencies are tasked with creating rules and regulations to advise other agencies and the public about how to comply with laws. These agencies are known as regulators and they can be thought of as the middle layer. There is a natural overlap between the top and middle layers as the federal regulators enforce privacy laws and penalties for those who break those laws. The bottom layer is self-regulation, where industry groups serve as both the regulators and the regulated. State attorneys general also work to enforce state privacy laws. Many states have enacted more stringent privacy protections than those currently found in federal laws to enforce consumer privacy. State attorneys general enforce these laws, and state privacy laws can be seen as an added level of protection that varies by state.

This chapter provides a general overview of major information privacy laws and regulators in the United States. Anyone seeking employment or working in one of these sectors should examine applicable laws more closely. The information privacy field and information privacy laws are continually changing as technology changes, as new privacy and security threats are indentified, and in response to global, market, and consumer demands. The following discussion of current laws lays the groundwork for further examination of these issues.

FEDERAL AGENCY REGULATORS

Given the sectoral approach that has been implemented over time in the United States, Congress has tasked many different federal agencies with crafting regulations to establish specific, focused rules and penalties and to engage in privacy law enforcement actions. Several federal agencies are involved in privacy policy making, including the Federal Trade Commission (FTC) and the Federal Communications Commission (FCC).[7] Under the provisions of some federal privacy laws, the FTC and the FCC are required to issue regulations. These regulations impose specific compliance requirements on those working within the private sector. When a covered entity fails to adhere to these requirements, these agencies may become involved to provide corrective guidance and enforce the regulations. Other federal agencies may also enforce privacy protections depending on the statutes or regulations that have been violated.

Trade and Marketing: The Federal Trade Commission

The FTC is a key agency enforcing consumer privacy protections as part of its larger focus on consumer protection. It is an independent agency that, under 15 U.S.C. § 45, is empowered to investigate and regulate "unfair and deceptive trade practices" and may bring enforcement actions.[8] The FTC's motto, prominently displayed on its website, is "protecting America's consumers." Part of the FTC's mission is to "prevent business practices that are anticompetitive or deceptive or unfair to consumers."[9]

The FTC is granted enforcement or administrative responsibilities under the following laws that specifically address consumer information privacy: the Fair Credit Reporting Act, the Gramm-Leach-Bliley Act, the Do Not Call Registry Act of 2003, the Fair and Accurate Credit Transactions Act of 2003, the Controlling the Assault of Non-Solicited Pornography and Marketing Act of 2003(CAN-SPAM Act), the Health Information Technology (HITECH) Act, provisions of American Recovery and Reinvestment Act of 2009, and sections of the Dodd-Frank Wall Street Reform and Consumer Protection Act of 2010.[10]

The FTC is empowered to pursue enforcement actions pursuant to federal statutes and may issue warnings or have a hearing presided over by an administrative judge. If a ruling is appealed, it may be reviewed in federal court. The FTC is also empowered to sue alleged violators in federal court. Under its power to investigate unfair and deceptive trade practices, the FTC has investigated and brought enforcement actions against many entities for privacy violations. The FCC shares enforcement responsibilities concerning telemarketing privacy and marketing related privacy rights with the Federal Trade Commission.

Several recent examples of FTC enforcement include the settlement concerning Google's rollout of its Buzz Social Network in 2010. The FTC charged that Google "used deceptive tactics and violated its own privacy promises to consumers when it launched its social network, Google Buzz" and enrolled some Gmail users who elected not to participate. The proposed 2011 settlement between the FTC and Google barred the company from future privacy misrepresentations and required it to implement a comprehensive privacy program along with independent privacy audits for the next twenty years.[11] However, Google was again the subject of an FTC investigation and settlement in 2012. Then Google agreed to pay a $22.5 million civil penalty, the largest the FTC has levied, to settle a claim that it again violated its privacy assurances, this time to users of Apple Inc.'s Safari Internet browser. Google had assured users that it would not place tracking cookies on their computers, which were set by default not to accept third-party cookies. It did place tracking cookies, and this violated not only Google's privacy assurances but also the earlier settlement. [12]

Business entities may and have sought guidance from the FTC prior to taking actions that may run afoul of the laws it enforces. The FTC issues advisory opinions on topics including consumer protection and privacy and on various proposed actions by entities. The FTC also issues warnings such as a 2013 warning it issued to 10 data-broker operations about possible privacy violations under the Fair Credit Reporting Act. [13] These opinions and warnings serve to assist in compliance with laws and regulations. [14]

Commerce, Trade, and Business Development: The U.S. Department of Commerce

The U.S. Department of Commerce has a focus on trade and works to improve U.S. commerce including trade, business development, and technology domestically and internationally. [15] As part of its international focus, the Department of Commerce developed a means for U.S. companies to comply with requirements for protecting personal data as set forth in the EU Directive 95/46/EC. The Safe Harbor certification program, which was approved by the EU and was designed to assist companies in the United States that process personal data from the EU, provides the means for organizations to comply with the protection requirements and maintain the privacy and integrity of the personal data that they process. Under the guidance of the Department of Commerce, U.S. companies can self-certify by adhering to certain principles. [16]

These principles include providing notice to individuals of how their data is being collected and used and providing them with the ability to opt-out of sharing this information with third parties and to opt-out of the collection of personal data. The transfer of personal data to third parties is limited to those parties that adhere to "adequate data protection principles." There is a requirement of access to the information being held by the organization and the right to correct or delete it if it is not accurate. There also must be a means to enforce these principles. [17] Both the FTC and the U.S. Department of Transportation can enforce actions against organizations that claim to be in compliance with the U.S.-EU Safe Harbor framework but are not. According to export.gov, other federal agencies and states, depending on the sector of the industry, can provide enforcement. [18] While the Safe Harbor program has enjoyed some success, recent revelations about NSA surveillance activities have raised concerns about the privacy and security of personal data from the EU. [19]

Finance: The Consumer Financial Protection Bureau, Federal Reserve Board, and Comptroller of Currency

Several agencies work to protect consumer financial interests. Chief among them is the Consumer Financial Protection Bureau (CFPB). The CFPB was established by provisions in the Dodd-Frank Wall Street Reform and Consumer Protection Act of 2010. It provides oversight to companies involved in consumer financial products and services. These include banks, credit unions, and financial companies.[20] The CFPB is not alone among federal regulators working to insure privacy and consumer protections among financial industries. The Federal Reserve Board and the Office of Comptroller of the Currency, an independent bureau of the U.S. Department of Treasury, also regulate financial institutions under the authority of the Gramm-Leach-Bliley Act.[21] These agencies have worked in part to improve the privacy notices financial institutions provide to consumers.[22]

Educational Records: The U.S. Department of Education

The U.S. Department of Education enforces the privacy rights of students at federally funded schools concerning their educational records. This is done under the authority of the Family Educational Rights and Privacy Act of 1974 (FERPA).[23] The department also promotes responsible data use and works to inform education policy and practices not covered by FERPA. It has initiated efforts to provide technical assistance directly to schools and at the state and school district level to help protect students' privacy rights. These initiatives reflect the department's commitment to upholding Fair Information Practice Principles (FIPPs).[24] In a 2011 statement about safeguarding student privacy, the department identified five core principles it was upholding: (1) Notice/Awareness (providing notice of information collection practices before collection); (2) Choice/Consent (giving the subjects of data collection options about whether and how their personal information may be used); (3) Access/Participation (providing access to an individual's personal information so that the individual can review and correct it); (4) Integrity/Security (the data collection process must include reasonable steps to make sure the data is accurate and secure); and (5) Enforcement/Redress (to be effective, there must be a mechanism for addressing and resolving complaints for failing to abide by the first four principles). FIPPs also provide guidance for government agency practice and regulation in the United States.[25] FIPPs and other information principles are addressed in greater depth in chapter 7.

Privacy in the Workplace: Equal Employment Opportunity Commission

Workplace privacy is addressed by the Equal Employment Opportunity Commission for issues concerning the Americans with Disabilities Act and other antidiscrimination statutes. Additional privacy protections for employees vary by state, though, in general, employees in the United States do not enjoy the same level of privacy protections as their European counterparts. Anyone working in human resources or with personal data concerning employees will want to familiarize themselves with workplace privacy issues at both the state and federal levels. The American Civil Liberties Union offers information concerning what privacy protections exist in the workplace. [26]

APPROACHES TO THE ENFORCEMENT OF PRIVACY RIGHTS

As noted above, some laws provide for a federal or state agency to bring enforcement actions against alleged violations. Others provide a private right of action for individuals to sue if their protected personal data has been used unlawfully or outside of the scope of what was agreed upon. For example, an individual might bring a civil suit for breach of contract when confidentiality is breached and the contract stipulated that personal data would remain confidential. In most states, one might also sue for invasion of privacy through misappropriation of name or likeness when these attributes are used for a commercial purpose without authorization and knowledge. [27]

A number of new and novel legal approaches are also being taken to stop privacy violations that the law has not kept pace with such as the "involuntary porn" or "revenge porn" online postings. These types of pornography postings feature pictures of nude individuals posted to websites without the permission of individuals in the photos and often identifying them. The pictures may be obtained through different means such as by a disgruntled ex-lover (revenge pornography) or through trickery, theft, or hacking (involuntary pornography). Some victims have turned to copyright law, asserting that they own the copyrights to the photos, as a basis to demand that those photos be taken down when efforts to seek assistance from police have been ineffective. [28] States are beginning to enact legislation to address this type of privacy violation, but many still lack adequate protections. [29]

STATE ATTORNEYS GENERAL AND STATE PRIVACY LAWS

In addition to the work of federal agencies, state attorneys general work to enforce their respective state's privacy protections of consumers. States have their own privacy laws that, in some instances, may be more comprehensive than existing federal laws. State attorneys general can bring privacy enforcement actions.

As noted in chapter 1, state constitutions can provide stronger privacy rights than those that are currently contained in the U.S. Constitution and statutes. The U.S. Constitution does not specifically contain the word *privacy*, but some state constitutions do. Alaska, Arizona, California, Florida, Hawaii, Illinois, Louisiana, Montana, South Carolina, and Washington state recognize a right of privacy in their state constitutions.[30] Where federal laws do not prevent it, state laws may impose stricter privacy requirements. Several states including California and Massachusetts are known for their strong stances on privacy protection. Increased concerns about privacy have led to the passage of "over two dozen privacy laws . . . in more than 10 states" in the past year.[31]

SELF-REGULATION

In the United States, there are a number of self-regulatory regimes that play a role in governing information privacy practices. Associations or groups provide guidance on accepted privacy practices for members of that association. While it is acknowledged that some efforts have been effective, a self-regulatory regime has not provided sufficient privacy protections for consumers. This has led to the passage of privacy laws and the establishment of enforcement powers for some federal agencies to protect consumer privacy.

PRIVACY LAWS BY SECTOR

Marketing and Telecommunications: TCPA, Do Not Call, CAN-SPAM

Some privacy-related issues to be aware of concerning telemarketing include restrictions on telephone and facsimile advertising. The Telephone Consumer Protection Act of 1991 (TCPA), which includes new provisions that came into effect in October 2013, was enacted to restrict "the making of telemarketing calls and the use of automatic telephone dialing systems and artificial or prerecorded voice messages."[32] Under the TCPA, faxes are also generally prohibited for advertising purposes unless there is an established business relationship between the sender and recipient.[33] In 2003, the National Do Not Call Registry was established. The National Do Not Call Registry allows consumers to register their residential and mobile phone numbers if they do not wish to receive calls from telemarketers. There are a few limitations to the National Do Not Call Registry. These permit "calls from or on behalf of political organizations, charities, and telephone surveyors" as well as "calls from companies with which you have an existing business relationship, or those to whom you've provided express agreement in writing to receive their calls."[34]

Changes to the TCPA effective October 16, 2013, place additional restrictions on the Do Not Call mandate. These changes address the use of automatic dialing systems or robo-dialers. They apply to both mobile and landline telephones. Under the revised TCPA, there must be written consent to telemarket with automatic dialers. The consumer must be informed clearly in the agreement that he or she will receive calls through an automatic dialing system and/or as a prerecorded voice message. Consumers must also be made aware that they do not have to consent to this type of telemarketing as a condition of the purchase of goods and services. This substantial change will impact the way that many businesses currently market to consumers.[35] It is important to understand the limitations placed on marketing when doing outreach efforts or marketing efforts for businesses. Some exceptions apply for emergencies, tax-exempt entities, and healthcare related messages. Those believing an exemption might apply to them should review the act and its changes.

Another key marketing limitation to be aware of is the Controlling the Assault of Non-Solicited Pornography and Marketing (CAN-SPAM) Act of 2003. This act applies to those marketing commercial content through electronic mail. While the law does not prohibit the sending of email advertising, it places parameters on these advertisements. According to "CAN-SPAM Act: A Compliance Guide for Business," if the primary purpose of the email is commercial advertising, it must meet seven requirements:

1. Headers must not be false or misleading.
2. Subject lines must not be deceptive.
3. You must disclose that the email is an advertisement.
4. The email must include a valid postal address.
5. Recipients must be told how they can opt-out.
6. Requests to opt-out must be handled promptly (within ten business days and without fee).
7. You must monitor what others are doing on your behalf in regards to email marketing. [36]

Other privacy protections for consumers are placed on telecommunications companies to limit their ability to access, use, and disclose personal data of consumers. These include the Telecommunications Act of 1996, which limits the access, use, and disclosure of customer proprietary network information.[37] This act applies to telecommunications carriers including phone companies. It also places limits on cable service providers concerning the use of personally identifiable information. A 1988 law, the Video Privacy

Protection Act, prohibits the disclosure of a consumer's movie-rental history. As this law has become somewhat outdated with the closing of video rental stores and the move to online rentals and streaming videos, an amendment to this law was passed to allow for easier methods to gain permission to allow the disclosure of rental histories.[38] This is of particular interest to companies such as Netflix and Facebook that may be able to use this information for marketing purposes.

Protecting Children and Teens Online—COPPA

Anyone working with commercial businesses with an online presence that may be of interest to children and will be collecting personal data should be familiar with 15 U.S.C. § 6501–6, the Children's Online Privacy Protection Act of 1998 (COPPA).[39] COPPA is a federal law designed to protect the privacy of children under the age of 13. It does so by regulating the collection and use of information provided by children under the age of 13 to commercial website operators. The Act, whose creation was sparked by concerns about the privacy of children on the Internet, applies to operators of commercial websites and online services including mobile apps. It also applies to websites that do not specifically target children but have "actual knowledge" that they are collecting information from children under the age of 13 and from "websites or online services that have actual knowledge that they are collecting personal information directly from users of another website or online service directed to children."[40]

Under the terms of COPPA, the FTC is required to issue and enforce regulations addressing children's online privacy. The FTC has provided a "Complying with COPPA: Frequently Asked Questions" page to answer questions that website operators and parents may have, and provides a means of corresponding with the FTC to follow-up questions if they are not addressed on the website. As the FTC revised its guidance concerning COPPA in July 2013, this page is especially useful to those seeking to understand the current requirements. According to the FTC's Bureau of Consumer Protection's Business Center, website operators covered by COPPA must adhere to the following seven rules for collecting and notifying users about the collection of personal data:

1. Post a clear and comprehensive online privacy policy describing their information practices for personal information collected online from children;
2. Provide direct notice to parents and obtain verifiable parental consent, with limited exceptions, before collecting personal information online from children;

3. Give parents the choice of consenting to the operator's collection and internal use of a child's information, but prohibiting the operator from disclosing that information to third parties (unless disclosure is integral to the site or service, in which case this must be made clear to parents);
4. Provide parents access to their child's personal information to review and/or have the information deleted;
5. Give parents the opportunity to prevent further use or online collection of a child's personal information;
6. Maintain the confidentiality, security, and integrity of information they collect from children, including by taking reasonable steps to release such information only to parties capable of maintaining its confidentiality and security; and
7. Retain personal information collected online from a child for only as long as is necessary to fulfill the purpose for which it was collected and delete the information using reasonable measures to protect against its unauthorized access or use. [41]

On November 14, 2013, a Senate bill was introduced to extend and revise COPPA to apply to children and "minors" under the age of 16. The new proposed law may be cited as the "Do Not Track Kids Act of 2013" and would prohibit the tracking, including location information, of youth without their consent. [42] This Act would apply to websites and mobile devices and has the potential to have a significant impact on business of many types. It is an area to keep an eye on for anyone working with mobile applications and websites that may be used by youth under age 16.

Education Records: Family Educational Rights and Privacy Act (FERPA) and the Protection of Pupil Rights Amendment (PPRA)

Anyone working in an education setting or with access to education records should be aware of the privacy protections provided by the Family Educational Rights and Privacy Act. Education records enjoy special privacy protections in the United States. FERPA provides protections for student education records by limiting the disclosure allowed without the student's consent. Disclosure without written consent is generally allowed for legitimate educational uses, health and safety emergencies, and state and local authorities to whom such disclosure is specifically allowed pursuant to state statute. [43] Directory information may be released without consent if students and parents are notified ahead of time and given a reasonable time to request that the information not be disclosed. This information may include the student's name, address, date and place of birth, dates of attendance, and any honors or awards. [44]

Under FERPA, students and the parents of students under the age of 18 have the right to review the student's education records and to request corrections of inaccuracies or misleading content. If the school does not amend the record, the student has a right to a hearing and to place a statement in the record presenting the student's view if no correction is made. Schools are required to notify students over age 18 or the parents of those under age 18 annually of their rights under FERPA.[45]

In 1978 FERPA was amended by the Protection of Pupil Rights Amendment (PPRA). PPRA applies to educational programs that receive funding from the U.S. Department of Education. It requires written consent from parents of minor children before those children participate in surveys, analyses, or evaluations that seek information about sensitive subjects such as:

1. Political affiliations or beliefs of the student or the student's parent;
2. Mental or psychological problems of the student or the student's family;
3. Sexual behavior or attitudes;
4. Illegal, antisocial, self-incriminating, or demeaning behavior;
5. Critical appraisals of other individuals with whom respondents have close family relationships;
6. Legally recognized privileged or analogous relationships, such as those of lawyers, physicians, and ministers;
7. Religious practices, affiliations, or beliefs of the student or student's parent; or
8. Income (other than that required by law to determine eligibility for participation in a program or for receiving financial assistance under such program). [46]

The protections of the PPRA were expanded by the No Child Left Behind Act of 2001. No Child Left Behind broadened the limits on collection and disclosure of sensitive information and requires federally funded elementary and secondary schools to enact policies regarding collection and disclosure, to allow parents access to inspect surveys, to provide notice of when activities are scheduled, and to provide parents with the right to opt-out of sharing student information for commercial purposes.[47]

Financial Records: Gramm-Leach-Bliley Act, Fair Credit Reporting Act

Individuals working in finance have long understood the importance of privacy with regard to financial records. Account numbers and other personally identifiable information must be protected as the costs of identity theft are high, and damage done to a consumer's credit rating can take years to repair.

A number of laws have been passed specifically to protect consumers engaging in financial transactions.

Private financial records are specifically protected. The Gramm-Leach-Bliley Act of 1999 requires financial institutions to protect the consumer information they collect. Under this act, financial institutions are also required to explain their information-sharing practices to customers.[48] More familiar to many readers is the Fair Credit Reporting Act (FCRA). FCRA was enacted in 1970 to ensure that consumer reporting agencies adopt reasonable procedures in credit reporting and provide consumers with the ability to access and correct the information about themselves contained within credit reports. This act also limits the use of consumer credit reports to certain "permissible purposes."[49] A 1996 amendment strengthened consumer rights to review and correct inaccuracies in their credit reports.[50]

The FCRA was amended by the Fair and Accurate Credit Transaction Act (FACT Act). The FACT Act was enacted in 2003 and is designed to help reduce identity theft and assist victims of this type of theft. The FACT Act requires that the three major credit reporting agencies (Equifax, Experian, and TransUnion) provide consumers with free copies of their credit reports every twelve months. This helps consumers to discover inaccuracies in the reports. It also allows consumers who fear they may have been the victim of credit fraud to place an alert in these files. Among the provisions designed to deter identity theft is a requirement that account numbers on credit card receipts be shortened[51] and, under the "red flags rule" many businesses are required to implement written identity theft prevention programs that are designed to detect identity theft and help prevent crime.[52]

As noted previously, the Dodd-Frank Wall Street Reform and Consumer Protection Act of 2010 created a new Consumer Financial Protection Bureau. The CFPB works to protect consumer financial interests from "unfair, deceptive, and abusive financial practices."[53] This mandate to protect against the "unfair" and the "deceptive" echoes that of the FTC and may apply to privacy protections for consumers engaged in certain financial transactions.[54]

Health Information: HIPAA, HITECH, and GINA

Doctors and other professional medical staff understand the importance of ensuring patient privacy as part of their professional duties. Others who may handle or come in contact with an individual's medical records may not share the same sense of professional duty to protect the privacy of individuals concerning medical procedures, diagnoses, and conditions. The Health Insurance Portability Act of 1996 (HIPAA) established a national standard for the protection of health information. Under HIPAA the "privacy rule" addresses how health information may be used and disclosed. The privacy rule is designed to balance privacy with the need to transmit health information.[55]

HIPAA applies to healthcare providers of all sizes, providers of health-care plans, and healthcare clearinghouses. When one of these "covered entities" uses a business or person to perform work involving protected health information, this business or person must also put in place privacy protections. [56] All individually identifiable health information is "protected health information." [57] It excludes information that has been de-identified; that is, it no longer identifies a specific individual.

HIPAA includes a security rule that addresses how personal health information must be secured including the administrative, technical, and physical safeguards that must be in place. HIPAA contains a requirement of notice of breach concerning protected health information. In 2009, a law was enacted that addresses privacy and security concerns associated with electronic health records. The Health Information Technology for Economic and Clinical Health (HITECH) Act strengthens the civil and criminal penalties for those who do not comply with HIPAA rules. [58] Similarly the Genetic Information Nondiscrimination Act (GINA) of 2008 was enacted to protect against genetic discrimination in health insurance and employment. GINA makes it illegal for an insurance company or employer to discriminate against an individual due to a genetic change that may increase the risk of an inherited disorder. [59]

Readers wanting to know more about HIPAA should consult the U.S. Department of Health and Hospitals, which offers many informative webpages to help parties identify whether or not they are covered entities and what their duties are under HIPAA. The site also provides useful information for consumers. [60] Individuals working in or seeking positions in almost any health-related service (i.e., hospitals, medical offices, benefits companies, laboratories, and agencies that review or do health research) will benefit from reviewing HIPAA's privacy and security requirements.

Government: FOIA, the Privacy Act, and the PATRIOT Act

Information professionals hold many positions in federal government agencies and with government contractors that require knowledge of privacy laws. These positions include but are not limited to government data librarians, information specialists, FOIA specialists, information privacy officers, and privacy analysts. Anyone seeking a career in information management in the federal sector should be familiar with the two main laws shaping federal government information privacy practice: the Privacy Act of 1974 [61] and the Freedom of Information Act.

The Privacy Act of 1974

The U.S. government collects, uses, and maintains large amounts of personally identifiable information. Much of this information is contained in systems of records that allow data to be searched and retrieved through the use of personal identifiers such as individuals' names or Social Security numbers. The Privacy Act of 1974 serves to regulate the government's collection, use, and disclosure of personal information contained in these systems. It allows individuals to review information about themselves and to amend or correct incorrect information. The Privacy Act of 1974 is applicable to all federal agencies, though some systems are exempt. Under the provisions of the Privacy Act, routine uses of personally identifiable information are allowed.[62] Routine uses include "the use of such record for a purpose which is compatible with the purpose for which it was collected."[63] Note the word *compatible*, which provides greater options for use than simply the purpose for which it was collected. This routine use might include the use of personally identifiable information to facilitate payments.

The Freedom of Information Act

The Freedom of Information Act (FOIA) provides individuals with a means to request information from the federal government. Under FOIA an individual may request from an executive branch department or agency any information that is not protected from public disclosure by one of nine exemptions or three special law enforcement record exclusions relating to law enforcement and national security. The nine exemptions permit the government to withhold:

1. Information classified to protect national security;
2. Information related solely to the internal personnel rules and practices of an agency;
3. Information that is prohibited from disclosure by another federal law;
4. Information concerning business trade secrets or other confidential commercial or financial information;
5. Information that concerns communications within or between agencies that are protected by legal privileges, that include but are not limited to:

    a. Attorney–work product privilege,
    b. Attorney–client privilege,
    c. Deliberative process privilege, and
    d. Presidential communications privilege;

6. Information that, if disclosed, would invade another individual's personal privacy;
7. Information compiled for law enforcement purposes if one of several specified types of harm would occur;
8. Information that concerns the supervision of financial institutions; and

9. Geological information on wells.[64]

Those wanting to know about FOIA are advised to visit the U.S. Department of Justice's website, which includes charts and figures of the number of FOIA requests received by federal agencies and more in-depth information about FOIA including how to make a FOIA request.

FISA, the PATRIOT Act, and NSLs: Terrorism Investigations That Impact Privacy and Protections

When the competing goals of privacy protection and terrorism investigation are both at play, our privacy protections may be compromised under the authority of the Foreign Intelligence Surveillance Act (FISA) of 1978[65] and the PATRIOT Act. Under FISA the government may conduct electronic surveillance to collect foreign intelligence in the United States. FISA establishes standards for the use of electronic surveillance, and government requests for FISA orders authorizing such surveillance are reviewed by a special court that reviews them in secret.

The government can also request information through the use of National Security Letters (NSLs). The Federal Bureau of Investigation (FBI) issues NSLs and can use them to demand information that it deems relevant to the gathering of foreign intelligence or the investigation of terrorism. NSLs contain a nondisclosure order, which means that information requested from entities and individuals through these letters must remain clandestine unless successfully challenged and the nondisclosure requirement is lifted.[66] The provisions and requirements for authorization of certain types of NSLs are provided for in several separate federal statutes.

Under the Right to Financial Privacy Act (RFPA),[67] which applies to personal financial information, NSLs are authorized. The Stored Communications Act, part of the Electronic Communications Privacy Act (ECPA), allows the use of NSLs to obtain electronic information including email and telephone information.[68] The FCRA authorizes the use of NSLs to obtain credit history information. The National Security Act of 1947 provides authority for the use of NSLs to investigate matters of national security.[69]

The USA PATRIOT Act,[70] formally known as the Uniting and Strengthening America by Providing Appropriate Tools Required to Intercept and Obstruct Terrorism Act of 2001, expanded the ability of the government to seek information under administrative subpoenas. The USA PATRIOT Act was signed into law on October 26, 2001, in the wake of the terrorist attacks of September 11. This Act expanded the powers of law enforcement for surveillance and investigation to deter terrorism. Its enforcement accordingly places limits on information privacy protection.

For example, information can be and has been requested from libraries using NSLs. The internet transaction records, loan history, and search history of library users are obtainable by the PATRIOT Act. Though often thought of in relation to libraries in library and information science circles, the PATRIOT Act may be used to obtain personal information from any type of information environment. Anyone working with personally identifiable information should be aware of FISA and the PATRIOT Act. The PATRIOT Act was renewed by President Obama in late May 2011 for another four years. It applies to people of all ages and is the authority cited by the NSA for the widespread surveillance of Americans. [71]

COSTS ASSOCIATED WITH INFORMATION BREACH

As noted above in the discussion of the Google settlement of $22.5 million, there can be substantial costs associated with privacy violations. In addition to the financial costs, there is detriment to the business's reputation. Private industry, corporations, businesses, and individuals, as well as federal agencies, need to maintain a level of trust both with individuals from whom they collect personally identifiable information and with those who they will want to keep as clients or users. Failing to ensure appropriate privacy measures, including adhering to privacy laws, regulations, and best practices, means that unhappy users may cease doing business with these entities or at least be less forthcoming with their personal information. It is not uncommon to hear that individuals use fake birthdays and maiden names to keep their personally identifiable information private.

Another cost associated with failure to abide by stated privacy policies, laws, and industry norms is that regulating agencies such as the FTC may impose multiyear monitoring and require the establishment of comprehensive privacy programs to address privacy violations and ensure that privacy protections are maintained in the future. These rehabilitative measures are more costly than planning for privacy security and incorporating it into the business's organizational structure and services.

CONCLUSION

The FTC plays an important role in regulating entities that use personally identifiable information. Together with other federal agencies such as the recently established Consumer Financial Protection Bureau, the Department of Commerce, and the Department of Education, the federal agencies monitor and protect information privacy in many venues while balancing the needs of business and commerce. Subject-specific federal laws protect personal information, and state laws provide additional privacy protections.

While the United States thus generally maintains a sectoral approach to privacy, protections continue to increase and change.

This discussion of privacy laws in the United States is not exhaustive. It serves as a starting point for understanding the information privacy environment. Those working in a particular industry or area are advised to read further about the information privacy issues that may be applicable in their work environments. State privacy laws for the state in which you work and any in which you and/or your employer do business should be reviewed. It should also be remembered that laws alone are not enough to ensure information privacy. Policies, practices, and privacy professionals all play an integral part in the protection of privacy. Information privacy requires vigilance and a dedication to remaining current on laws, practices, policies, technology, and training for all.

NOTES

1. *Personally identifiable information* and *personal data* are used interchangeably in this chapter to refer to any information relating to an identified or identifiable natural person. For more on the subject of personally identifiable information see chapter 1 and the glossary of this book.

2. Directive 95/46/EC of the European Parliament and of the Council of October 24, 1995, on the protection of individuals with regard to the processing of personal data and on the free movement of such data, 1995, http://eur-lex.europa.eu/LexUriServ/LexUriServ.do?uri=CELEX:31995L0046:en:HTML (accessed October 28, 2013).

3. The Guardian, "The NSA Files," 2013, www.theguardian.com/world/the-nsa-files (accessed October 28, 2013); Electronic Frontier Foundation, "NSA Spying on Americans," www.eff.org/nsa-spying (accessed October 28, 2013).

4. Council on Foreign Relations, "Global Responses to NSA Surveillance: Three Things to Know," October 25, 2013, www.cfr.org/intelligence/global-responses-nsa-surveillance-three-things-know/p31728; NBCNews.com, "US Coping with Furious Allies as NSA Spying Revelations Grow," October 28, 2013, http://usnews.nbcnews.com/_news/2013/10/28/21209499-us-coping-with-furious-allies-as-nsa-spying-revelations-grow?lite; FoxNews.com, "Report Claims NSA Monitored 60 Million Phone Calls in Spain," October 28, 2013, www.foxnews.com/politics/2013/10/28/report-claims-nsa-monitored-60-million-phone-calls-in-spain; James Ball, "NSA Monitored Calls of 35 World Leaders after US Official Handed Over Contacts," *The Guardian*, October 24, 2013, www.theguardian.com/world/2013/oct/24/nsa-surveillance-world-leaders-calls.

5. Deb Riechmann, Associated Press, "NSA Spying Threatens to Undermine US Foreign Policy; Obama, Kerry Try to Quell Furor Abroad," *Star Tribune*, October 26, 2013, www.startribune.com/politics/national/229355621.html.

6. "Legislation," in *Black's Law Dictionary*, 6th ed. (St. Paul, MN: West Publishing, 1991).

7. Other agencies involved in federal privacy policy making include the U.S. Department of Commerce, the U.S. Office of Management and Budget, and the U.S. Department of Justice. Several agencies are empowered to enforce actions based on breach of privacy including the Office of Civil Rights of the U.S. Department of Health and Human Services for violations under the Health Insurance Portability and Accountability Act.

8. Section 5 of the FTC Act, 15 U.S.C. § 45, prohibits "unfair or deceptive acts or practices." The full text of this act is available at www.gpo.gov/fdsys/pkg/USCODE-2011-title15/pdf/USCODE-2011-title15-chap2-subchapI-sec45.pdf.

9. "About the Federal Trade Commission," *Federal Trade Commission*, October 17, 2013, www.ftc.gov/ftc/about.shtm (accessed November 4, 2013).

10. "Legal Resources—Statutes Relating to Consumer Protection Mission," *Federal Trade Commission*, June 28, 2012, www.ftc.gov/ogc/stat3.shtm (accessed November 4, 2013).

11. "FTC Charges Deceptive Privacy Practices in Google's Rollout of Its Buzz Social Network," *Federal Trade Commission*, March 30, 2011, www.ftc.gov/opa/2011/03/google.shtm.

12. "Google Will Pay $22.5 Million to Settle FTC Charges It Misrepresented Privacy Assurances to Users of Apple's Safari Internet Browser," *Federal Trade Commission*, August 9, 2012, www.ftc.gov/opa/2012/08/google.shtm.

13. "FTC Warns Data Broker Operations of Possible Privacy Violations," *Federal Trade Commission*, May 7, 2013, www.ftc.gov/opa/2013/05/databroker.shtm.

14. "Advisory Opinions," *Federal Trade Commission*, April 19, 2013, www.ftc.gov/ftc/opinions.shtm.

15. "Mission Statement," U.S. Department of Commerce, www.commerce.gov/about-department-commerce (accessed October 31, 2013).

16. "eTrust Safe Harbor program," U.S. Department of Commerce, 2012–2013, www.etrust.org/safeharbor/index.html (accessed October 31, 2013).

17. Ibid.

18. "U.S.-EU Safe Harbor," Export.gov, July 1, 2013, http://export.gov/safeharbor/eu/eg_main_018476.asp.

19. Jennifer Baker, "Data Privacy Concerns Could Derail EU-US Trade Talks," PCWorld, October 29, 2013, www.pcworld.com/article/2058921/data-privacy-concerns-could-derail-euus-trade-talks.html.

20. "About Us," Consumer Financial Protection Bureau, www.consumerfinance.gov/the-bureau (accessed November 13, 2013).

21. "About the OCC," Office of the Comptroller of the Currency, www.occ.gov/about/what-we-do/mission/index-about.html (accessed November 13, 2013).

22. "Federal Regulators Seek Public Comment on Ways to Improve Privacy Notices," The Federal Reserve Board, December 23, 2003, www.federalreserve.gov/BoardDocs/Press/bcreg/2003/20031223/default.htm.

23. 20 U.S.C. § 1232g, www.gpo.gov/fdsys/pkg/USCODE-2012-title20/pdf/USCODE-2012-title20-chap31-subchapIII-part4-sec1232g.pdf.

24. "U.S. Department of Education Safeguarding Student Privacy," United States Department of Education, www2.ed.gov/policy/gen/guid/fpco/ferpa/safeguarding-student-privacy.pdf (accessed November 14, 2013).

25. "Fair Information Practice Principles," Federal Trade Commission, November 23, 2012, www.ftc.gov/reports/privacy3/fairinfo.shtm.

26. "Workplace Privacy," American Civil Liberties Union, www.aclu.org/technology-and-liberty/workplace-privacy (accessed November 15, 2013).

27. "False Light—Misappropriation—Right of Publicity," Reporters Committee for the Freedom of the Press, May 6, 2014, www.rcfp.org/first-amendment-handbook/false-light-misappropriation-right-publicity.

28. Lorelei Laird, "Victims Are Taking on 'Revenge Porn' Websites for Posting Photos They Didn't Consent To," *American Bar Association Magazine*, November 2013, www.abajournal.com/magazine/article/victims_are_taking_on_revenge_porn_websites_for_posting_photos_they_didnt_c. Also see the website *Without My Consent* for more information on legal options for victims of online harassment, www.withoutmyconsent.org (accessed October 30, 2013).

29. As of February 2014, Georgia, Illinois, Maryland, Pennsylvania, and Virginia are considering legislation to protect against revenge porn. The House of Delegates of Virginia passed a bill to outlaw revenge porn. These states may follow in the lead of California (2013) and New Jersey (2004), who both passed laws to protect against this most intimate invasion of privacy. See Tal Koplan, "States Criminalize 'Revenge Porn,'" Politico, October 30, 2013, www.politico.com/story/2013/10/states-criminalize-revenge-porn-99082.html?hp=l9.

30. "Privacy Protections in State Constitutions," National Conference of State Legislatures, 2013, www.ncsl.org/research/telecommunications-and-information-technology/privacy-protections-in-state-constitutions.aspx (accessed October 28, 2013).

31. Somini Sengupta, "No U.S. Action, So States Move on Privacy Law," *New York Times*, October 30, 2013, available online at www.nytimes.com/2013/10/31/technology/no-us-action-so-states-move-on-privacy-law.html?_r=0&pagewanted=print.

32. "Telemarketing Policy," Federal Communications Commission, November 30, 2012, http://transition.fcc.gov/cgb/policy/telemarketing.html.

33. "Fax Advertising: What You Need to Know," Federal Communications Commission, www.fcc.gov/guides/fax-advertising (accessed November 15, 2013).

34. "National Do Not Call Registry," Federal Trade Commission, September 2009, www.consumer.ftc.gov/articles/0108-national-do-not-call-registry.

35. Duane Morris LLP, "New TCPA Rules Effective October 16, 2013," Martindale.com, September 27, 2013, www.martindale.com/communications-law/article_Duane-Morris-LLP_1976018.htm.

36. "CAN-SPAM Act: A Compliance Guide for Business," Federal Trade Commission, September 2009, http://business.ftc.gov/documents/bus61-can-spam-act-compliance-guide-business.

37. The certified full-text version of the Telecommunications Act of 1996 is available through the U.S. Government Printing Office at www.gpo.gov/fdsys/pkg/PLAW-104publ104/pdf/PLAW-104publ104.pdf.

38. A certified copy of the 2012 amendment is available from the U.S. Government Printing Office at www.gpo.gov/fdsys/pkg/BILLS-112hr6671enr/pdf/BILLS-112hr6671enr.pdf. More information concerning the history of the Video Privacy Protection Action can be found at http://epic.org/privacy/vppa/.

39. "The Children's Online Privacy Protection Act of 1998," Federal Trade Commission, www.ftc.gov/ogc/coppa1.htm (accessed October 29, 2013).

40. "Complying with COPPA: Frequently Asked Questions: A Guide for Business and Parents and Small Entity Compliance Guide," Federal Trade Commission, July 2013, www.business.ftc.gov/documents/Complying-with-COPPA-Frequently-Asked-Questions.

41. Ibid. at "A. General Questions about the COPPA Rule."

42. Cecilia Kang, "Bills Would Curb Tracking of and Advertising to Children on Internet," *Washington Post*, November 14, 2013, available online at www.washingtonpost.com/business/technology/bills-would-curb-tracking-of-and-advertising-to-children-on-internet/2013/11/14/dee03382-4d58-11e3-ac54-aa84301ced81_story.html.

43. 20 U.S.C. § 1232g, www.gpo.gov/fdsys/pkg/USCODE-2012-title20/pdf/USCODE-2012-title20-chap31-subchapIII-part4-sec1232g.pdf.

44. "Family Educational Rights and Privacy Act (FERPA)," U.S. Department of Education, www.ed.gov/policy/gen/guid/fpco/ferpa/index.html (accessed November 15, 2013).

45. Ibid.

46. 20 U.S. Code § 1232h—"Protection of Pupil Rights."

47. No Child Left Behind (NCLB) Act of 2001, Pub. L. No. 107-110, § 115, Stat. 1425 (2002).

48. The Bureau of Consumer Protection provides information for institutions on how to comply with the Gramm-Leach-Bliley Act as well as helpful information for consumers at http://business.ftc.gov/privacy-and-security/gramm-leach-bliley-act.

49. The complete text of the Fair Credit Reporting Act (FCRA), 15 U.S.C. § 1681 et seq., is available at www.ftc.gov/os/statutes/031224fcra.pdf.

50. A version of the FCRA with amendments including those set forth in the Consumer Credit Reporting Reform Act of 1996, the Consumer Reporting Employment Clarification Act of 1998, section 506 of the Gramm-Leach-Bliley Act, the USA PATRIOT Act, the Fair and Accurate Credit Transactions Act of 2003, the Consumer Financial Protection Act of 2010 and others as prepared by the staff of the Federal Trade Commission is available at www.ftc.gov/os/statutes/031224fcra.pdf.

51. "Provisions of New Fair and Accurate Credit Transactions Act Will Help Reduce Identity Theft and Help Victims Recover: FTC," Federal Trade Commission, June 15, 2004, www.ftc.gov/opa/2004/06/factaidt.shtm.

52. "Fighting Identity Theft with the Red Flags Rule: A How-To Guide for Business," Federal Trade Commission, May 2013, www.business.ftc.gov/documents/bus23-fighting-identity-theft-red-flags-rule-how-guide-business.

53. "Creating the Consumer Financial Protection Bureau," Consumer Financial Protection Bureau, www.consumerfinance.gov/the-bureau/creatingthebureau (accessed November 15, 2012).

54. Peter P. Swire and Kenesa Ahmad, *U.S. Private-Sector Privacy: Law and Practice for Information Privacy Professional* (Portsmouth, NH: International Association of Privacy Professionals, 2012), 72.

55. "OCR Privacy Brief: Summary of the HIPAA Privacy Rule," U.S. Department of Health and Human Services, May 2003, www.hhs.gov/ocr/privacy/hipaa/understanding/summary/privacysummary.pdf, 1.

56. Ibid., 2–3.

57. Ibid., 3–4.

58. "HITECH Act Enforcement Interim Final Rule," U.S. Department of Health and Human Services, www.hhs.gov/ocr/privacy/hipaa/administrative/enforcementrule/hitechenforcementifr.html (accessed February 23, 2014).

59. Pub. L.110 - 233, 122 Stat. 881 (2008), Genetic Information Nondiscrimination Act of 2008.

60. "Health Information Privacy," U.S. Department of Health and Human Services, www.hhs.gov/ocr/privacy/hipaa/understanding/index.html (accessed November 15, 2013).

61. The Privacy Act of 1974 is available through the U.S. Department of Justice website at www.justice.gov/opcl/privstat.htm.

62. "Privacy Act of 1974, as Amended," Federal Trade Commission, November 30, 2010, www.ftc.gov/foia/privacy_act.shtm.

63. Ibid., subsection (a)(7).

64. "Frequently Asked Questions," U.S. Department of Justice, February 2011, www.foia.gov/faq.html#exemptions.

65. The Foreign Intelligence Surveillance Act (FISA) 50 U.S.C. §§ 1801–11 (1978).

66. Charles Doyle, *National Security Letters in Foreign Intelligence Investigations: A Glimpse at the Legal Background*, U.S. Library of Congress, Congressional Research Service, CRS Report RS22406 (Washington, DC: Office of Congressional Information and Publishing, 2014).

67. The Right to Financial Privacy Act (RFPA), 12 U.S.C. § 3414 (1978).

68. The Electronic Communications Privacy Act (ECPA), 18 U.S.C. § 2709; Charles Doyle, *Privacy: An Overview of the Electronic Communications Privacy Act*, U.S. Library of Congress, Congressional Research Service, CRS Report R41733 (Washington, DC: Office of Congressional Information and Publishing, 2012), available online at www.fas.org/sgp/crs/misc/R41733.pdf.

69. The National Security Act , 50 U.S.C. § 436. "National Security Letters," Electronic Privacy Information Center, http://epic.org/privacy/nsl (accessed March 15, 2014).

70. The full text of the PATRIOT Act, is available through the U.S. Government Printing Office at www.gpo.gov/fdsys/pkg/PLAW-107publ56/pdf/PLAW-107publ56.pdf.

71. Brett Max Kaufman, "ACLU Files Lawsuit Challenging NSA's Patriot Act Phone Surveillance," ACLU.org, June 11, 2013, www.aclu.org/blog/national-security-technology-and-liberty/aclu-files-lawsuit-challenging-nsas-patriot-act-phone.

BIBLIOGRAPHY

Bachman, Katy. "Government Report Calls for Comprehensive Privacy Law: Consumers Should Have More Information, Control over Personal Data." November 20, 2013.

www.adweek.com/news/technology/government-report-calls-comprehensive-privacy-law-153996.

"Complying with COPPA: Frequently Asked Questions: A Guide for Business and Parents and Small Entity Compliance Guide." Federal Trade Commission, July 2013. www.business.ftc.gov/documents/Complying-with-COPPA-Frequently-Asked-Questions.

Doyle, Charles. *National Security Letters in Foreign Intelligence Investigations: A Glimpse at the Legal Background.* U.S. Library of Congress, Congressional Research Service. CRS Report RS22406. Washington, DC: Office of Congressional Information and Publishing, 2014.

———. *Privacy: An Overview of the Electronic Communications Privacy Act.* U.S. Library of Congress, Congressional Research Service. CRS Report R41733. Washington, DC: Office of Congressional Information and Publishing, 2012). Available online at www.fas.org/sgp/crs/misc/R41733.pdf.

Kang, Cecilia. "Bills Would Curb Tracking of and Advertising to Children on Internet." *The Washington Post*, November 14, 2013. www.washingtonpost.com/business/technology/bills-would-curb-tracking-of-and-advertising-to-children-on-internet/2013/11/14/dee03382-4d58-11e3-ac54-aa84301ced81_story.html.

Kaufman, Brett Max. "ACLU Files Lawsuit Challenging NSA's Patriot Act Phone Surveillance." ACLU.org, June 11, 2013. www.aclu.org/blog/national-security-technology-and-liberty/aclu-files-lawsuit-challenging-nsas-patriot-act-phone.

"National Security Letters." Electronic Privacy Information Center, http://epic.org/privacy/nsl (accessed March 15, 2014).

"Privacy Protections in State Constitutions." National Conference of State Legislatures, 2013. www.ncsl.org/research/telecommunications-and-information-technology/privacy-protections-in-state-constitutions.aspx (accessed October 28, 2013).

Sengupta, Somini. "No U.S. Action, So States Move on Privacy Law." *New York Times*, October 30, 2013. www.nytimes.com/2013/10/31/technology/no-us-action-so-states-move-on-privacy-law.html?_r=0&pagewanted=print.

Swire, Peter P., and Kenesa Ahmad. *U.S. Private-Sector Privacy: Law and Practice for Information Privacy Professionals.* Portsmouth, NH: International Association of Privacy Professionals, 2012.

Chapter Four

Privacy Literacy

The term *privacy literacy* is used here to identify one's level of understanding and awareness of how information is tracked and used in online environments, and how that information can retain or lose its private nature.[1] Promoting a high level of privacy literacy generally is important to commercial and social organizations and to individuals. If each person online has a different understanding of information privacy and is either unaware or unconcerned about how information can or should be captured and used, their varied privacy values and online practices will inevitably diminish information privacy to the detriment of all. Education and continuing training are crucial to help ensure a baseline understanding of information privacy for all and to minimize risks in information environments.

While the focus of the discussion that follows is primarily about developing privacy literacy through privacy education and awareness of privacy risks in online environments, individuals should use caution in releasing personal information in all environments. It is prudent to always question whether all the requested personal information is needed to perform a task or receive a service. If there is any doubt as to the necessity of the collection of personal information, the individual or entity seeking the information should be questioned about why the information is needed and how it will be safeguarded. Each of us must make our own information privacy a priority. Developing privacy literacy can help in that endeavor.

DIGITAL LITERACY

Privacy literacy goes hand in hand with digital literacy. The ALA Digital Technology Taskforce defines *digital literacy* as

the ability to use information and communication technologies to find, evaluate, create, and communicate information, requiring both cognitive and technical skills.[2]

If an individual does not understand the risks he or she takes when searching,
accessing websites, and providing information online, that person cannot
accurately evaluate the value of the information. If the cost of access is not
known, then the value of the information obtained cannot accurately be
measured. Users must evaluate whether it is worth trading some of their
privacy to obtain information from a website. They must consider how much
information is being collected, what it will be used for, and with whom it will
be shared.

In order to realistically evaluate the degree to which an individual's private information may be exposed, each user needs to become "literate" about
how such personal information may be collected and used. Individuals need
to understand how their online movements can be tracked and used by the
service providers. Users must be able to make informed decisions when
balancing the value of a resource against the possible loss of privacy that
could occur when using it.

The relationship between privacy literacy and digital literacy is referenced in the ALA Digital Literacy Taskforce's assessment that a digitally
literate individual understands the relationship between technology and "personal privacy."[3] Privacy literacy encompasses this position and expands the
competency to incorporate understanding the practical and ethical trade-offs
individuals make when they seek and obtain information as well as the mechanisms by which personal privacy can be compromised, how personal information may be used, and how individuals can protect themselves.

INFORMATION LITERACY

The Association of College and Research Libraries (ACRL) has produced its
Information Literacy Competency Standards for Higher Education. In it, the
ACRL references the final report of the ALA's Presidential Committee on
Information Literacy, defining *information literacy* as

> A set of abilities requiring individuals to "recognize when information is
> needed and have the ability to locate, evaluate, and use effectively the needed
> information."[4]

The ACRL's standards address information literacy's relationship to information technology, finding that individuals who develop information literacy
"necessarily develop some technology skills." Understanding safe online in-

formation privacy practices is a necessary complement to these technology skills.

Understanding information privacy threats and safe online privacy practices when seeking information or doing business in an online environment should be mandatory for everyone as we continue to move forward in a global society that relies heavily on digital content and where a great deal of business is conducted online. Users of digital devices need to understand that when they enter the digital environment they leave behind a trail of data known as a digital. Individuals seeking and evaluating information online in a work environment, in a school setting, in libraries, and even in the privacy of their own homes need to understand how personal information about them is being gathered and used.

PRIVACY EDUCATION FOR ONLINE USERS

Librarians and other information professionals are likely to encounter adult patrons, youth, and fellow employees who will need guidance on safe online information privacy practices. Understanding the differences in their motivation, skill, and the unique aspects of the information environments in which they are seeking information can help in tailoring information privacy education to each group's needs.

Patrons

Patrons of public libraries run the gambit from computer savvy to novices. The wide economic, educational, cultural, and age differences of patrons means that the library will serve both those who understand how to access information and safeguard their privacy while online and others who need assistance with basic web searching, word processing, evaluating information found on the web, and judging the trustworthiness of websites. Jeannette Woodward identifies two particularly vulnerable groups: immigrants and adults from low-income households. Immigrants may not be as familiar with the English language and therefore may more easily fall victim to online and email scams. Individuals from low-income households may not have the same opportunities to practice their digital literacy skills and may be more vulnerable online for this reason.[5]

Youth

Youth of varying ages, education, and backgrounds have different expectations about privacy and some may feel so comfortable sharing information that they could pose privacy risks to themselves and others. Children are naturally less likely to know and understand the privacy implications and are more likely to share information presuming it will remain secure. This, in turn, attracts the attention of online predators and invites unwanted attention, ridicule, or other adverse consequences.[6] Librarians are uniquely placed to assist children and young adults in developing information literacy skills and in teaching safe web practices. On a daily basis youth visit school and public libraries where the professionals have opportunities to assist them in gaining a greater understanding of the privacy issues and safe privacy practices. Learning safe online privacy practices while still in school will help children and young adults now and for a lifetime.

Focus should be placed on training youth about the dangers of sharing information on social networking sites and gaming environments, as well as sharing information generally to enter contests or gain access to sites. Youth should be made aware of the many ways that information can be gathered through online interactions, including friends' postings that may be used for nefarious purposes. They should be instructed about how they can protect their information, including the use of passwords and aliases. There are many sources online, including YouTube videos, games, cartoons, and graphic novels that can help instruct children about the perils of sharing information online. Some particularly good sources include a graphic novel created by the Office of the Privacy Commissioner of Canada and an interactive pirate game created by Media Smarts, Canada's Centre for Digital and Media Literacy.[7]

Employees

Employees who are not privacy "literate" represent a vulnerability for businesses. They may compromise privacy and security measures and expose personal or confidential information without realizing it. Employee online access rights can and should be limited to what each employee needs to perform his or her job. However, while physical barriers, firewalls, passwords, and other security measures are useful, for most organizations access to large amounts of sensitive information by employees is necessary to do business. The key to ensuring employee adherence to privacy and security measures is to educate them and to develop a practice of ongoing education and other opportunities for reinforcement of the role that all employees play in securing critical information privacy by adhering to proper privacy and security protocols. Employees may have differing levels of access to information, but all should understand the importance of protecting private or confidential information and how their actions affect the security of this information. The very nature of private or commercially confidential information means that it should not be made publicly available.

Training should be customized to the needs of the business unit or type of work being performed. Linking information privacy and security to the goals and strategic plan of the entity, and explaining the value of ensuring the safety of PII to the economic and reputational health of the entity will raise awareness of the importance of keeping current on privacy and security best practices. Incorporating regular privacy and security training and assessments into employees' performance plans and appraisals can help ensure that privacy and security remain high priorities.

INFORMATION GATHERING ONLINE

When we search online for information, shop, visit websites, and chat or post information without taking precautions, our private information is especially vulnerable. Many different parties are interested in obtaining and using our personal information. We may not even be aware that we are giving this information away. While there is not time or space here to discuss all types of online information gathering, the following are some of the primary mechanisms available.

Cookies and Web Beacons

Cookies are small text files that are placed by websites onto our computers to allow web servers to store information there. This information is often used to enhance our experience when using the website, but they also act to collect data. To keep privacy protections high, it is wise to browse in your computer's highest privacy and security modes that will still allow you to surf the Internet and perform needed online transactions. Setting cookies to delete every time a user finishes a browsing session is helpful in managing privacy.

Local shared objects, also known as "flash cookies" are another means by which web servers store their information on a user's computer. Flash cookies allow for the depositing of more complex data through the use of Adobe's Flash plug-in.[8] The user's storage and deletion of flash cookies must be done in Adobe Flash's Settings Manager. It is recommended that anyone using Flash Player examine their privacy settings, delete unwanted flash cookies, and manage the privacy rights settings for access to your computer cameras and microphones by websites that have been previously visited and for which flash cookies may have been deposited.[9]

Web beacons, also called web bugs and sometimes clear GIFs, are usually invisible bits of html embedded in email messages or websites. When embedded in emails by spammers, they can be used to verify that email addresses are legitimate. Clicking on one can lead to more incoming spam.[10] Web beacons can identify whether someone has opened an email, or they may be used to determine who is browsing a webpage and the browser's behavior. They are often used in conjunction with cookies. The use of web beacons allows for more uninvited targeted marketing of users. Third parties may also use beacons to track behavioral information about an online browser. It is therefore recommended that, whenever feasible, settings be configured to not allow cookies so that there is less information for beacons to identify.

Yahoo explains that it might collect information using web beacons to identify users' "traffic patterns," so as to understand how they use products and services, and then report the traffic pattern data to Yahoo advertisers. Though Yahoo asserts that "no personally identifiable information about you is shared with our advertisers and other partners as part of these services,"[11] that is no guarantee that advertisers need that PII from Yahoo in order to mine and connect information to identify users.

Internet Protocol (IP) Addresses

Our Internet Protocol (IP) addresses are used to identify our computers or our routers, if we are part of a network, when we connect to the Internet. The IP address provides specific location information necessary for data transfer. However, it can also provide information that identifies our general physical location or the location of the router. The Internet service provider (ISP) can provide a more specific physical address if requested by law enforcement.

While the sharing of an IP address may not be much of a concern to most of us when thinking about privacy, the sharing of other information that we consider private poses greater risks. Recent information has come to light about the NSA scanning our emails and examining our searches without the need of a warrant. The contents of our private emails and searches contain information that we have not agreed to share. This personal information can be linked to us through our email addresses and our IP addresses, which provide a physical location.

Data Mining

Data mining is a process of analyzing large volumes of data for patterns and connections. Data mining is often done with the help of software that makes it possible to analyze large volumes of data. Though data mining has been beneficial to us in many ways, including allowing researchers to determine patterns of the spread of disease and helping to keep spam from clogging our inboxes, some aspects of data mining cause concern. Through the analyses of IP addresses and other information, data miners have been able to re-identify[12] individuals whose data had been anonymized. According to the Electronic Privacy Information Center (EPIC), this type of data mining is often done by third parties without the consent or awareness of consumers. EPIC references two studies that have shown that by combining information from as few as two different datasets, re-identification can be achieved. A 1990 study showed that information from the census data "could be combined to uniquely identify 87% of the United States population."[13] These studies highlight the significance of the problem of mass data collection and the lack of control individuals have over their own personal data.

Data mining continues to be widely used. Even government agencies are using data-mining strategies to learn more about individuals and to link the information known about individuals and contained in databases across agencies. There are many companies and individuals who are anxious to gather more data for marketing, to sell our data to others, to spy on us, to create mischief, or for reasons we may not be aware of.

Search Logs and Email Scanning

Search logs[14] can be especially revealing as many people search their own names and the names of friends and relatives. The contents of the search queries create a fuller picture of the searcher, but without context or explanation, they can also create false impressions. A search might be performed about cancer but not reveal if the searcher is looking on his or her own behalf, for a family member, or just to satisfy curiosity. Erroneous assumptions can easily be made.

A classic example of how an erroneous assumption could be made from search queries was featured in the documentary film about the loss of privacy on the Internet titled *Terms and Conditions May Apply*.[15] The director, Cullen Hoback, looked at how the search queries of a writer about dead bodies and killing your wife might lead one to believe that his wife was in imminent danger. Closer investigation reveals that he is a screenwriter. This would also explain his ability to search for food in between the focused searches about murder.

Knowing that the NSA is examining search logs and the contents of emails, the question for many becomes, *Why is the NSA searching through our private searches and correspondence?* The answer so far has been that the NSA was acting for national and global security. If this is the case, does it mean that local law enforcement is also reading our email and search logs? Caitlin Dewey, writing for the *Washington Post*, sought to answer this question. She consulted Hanni Fakhoury, a staff attorney at the Electronic Frontier Foundation, for advice. According to Mr. Fakhoury, local law enforcement always needs probable cause.[16] Unless they can make a showing of good cause, it is unlikely that local law enforcement will read about your weekend plans.

Social Media Posts

While much of what we do on social media sites may seem harmless, taken together it builds a profile about each of us. Information can be connected across platforms to present what is sometimes a skewed portrait of our interests, political beliefs, financial or health situations, and more. Social networking sites in particular are mined for information by advertisers, political groups, and potential employers, among others. It is important to think carefully about posting any personal information that can easily be copied and shared. Additionally, anyone posting pictures should consider how they might be viewed by future employers and others. It should also be considered that information about you may be generated by friends and you may be tagged in pictures. Each of us is responsible for working to secure our own privacy and that of others as we post and comment online. It is prudent to pause and consider the ramifications of actions before posting. Once that information is out there, it may never truly be removed or controlled.

Tweets are just one example of the permanence of online posts. Research is being conducted about posts on sites such as Twitter[17] to determine the impact of news and ideas. Given reports that tweets are being archived by the Library of Congress,[18] what you tweet can last beyond your lifetime. The length of time that information one posts online remains available is indefinite.

Online Gaming

Caution also should be used when revealing personal information in online gaming and in posting or sharing information in general. Gamers do not always know who they are playing with or how information revealed in online chats will be used. Tensions can run high in online games, and posts may be made in haste that can have lasting negative effects.

ENHANCING PRIVACY ONLINE

While it might seem like the most basic advice, and therefore unnecessary to give, anyone advising others in online privacy should recommend that all web browsing be done at the highest privacy and security levels feasible for their needs. Users seeking to maintain privacy should ideally block all cookies. However, such a plan is unfeasible for viewing and using the features of many websites. Therefore, users will want to set their privacy settings high enough that they block cookies that could save the user's contact information without obtaining their explicit consent and do not have a compact privacy policy. It is also recommended that pop-up blockers be activated. Users should not accept automatic downloading from potentially unsafe sites or the automatic downloading of unsigned ActiveX controls.[19]

Phishing and Passwords

Links sent to a user in emails should be carefully considered and, if necessary, independently investigated. Most reputable websites with whom you do business will never send you an email asking for account information, and users should even be wary of notices reporting an account breach and providing a link to click to reset a password. Users should always be advised to consider carefully the likelihood that these are "phishing" scams, and proceed with caution. Along the same lines, users should be advised that links containing tiny URLs (shortened URL addresses) have been used by hackers to spoof legitimate sites. Therefore, unless you are certain about the origins of the link, it is advisable to refrain from clicking on it.

Passwords are a form of self-authentication; they should be carefully secured and not shared with others. Creating strong passwords is important to ensuring the security of a user's information. Strong passwords are created using a combination of upper- and lowercase letters, numbers, and, where permitted, symbols. Tempting though it may be, users should avoid using the same password for multiple sites, sharing passwords with family or friends, and using familiar names or numbers as part of their passwords (user's own name, names of pets, familiar locations, birthdates, addresses, adjacent keys). Weak passwords can allow hackers access to email accounts, online bank and shopping accounts, and personal information stored there. Once a password has been compromised, it can be used to access other accounts if the same password is used for more than one account. Passwords should be changed periodically and users who have difficulty managing passwords may want to invest in password-manager software.

Public Wi-Fi Hotspots

Public Wi-Fi is available in many areas and can often be found in public libraries, schools, bookstores, airports, and coffee shops. What may at first seem to be a valuable perk poses privacy and security risks that should be considered when using public Wi-Fi. One risk is that your information may be intercepted. Public Wi-Fi is often unencrypted and therefore susceptible to tampering. If you are using a Wi-Fi service that is not encrypted, you should avoid sending personal information. Even logging in to your e-mail account is not recommended as your account may be compromised unless the e-mail website is fully encrypted.

The FTC in conjunction with the Department of Homeland Security administers a website called OnGuardOnline.gov. Visitors to this website will find information to help them ensure online security including tips for using unencrypted Wi-Fi hotspots such as signing out of online accounts promptly when not in active use by the account owner. Remaining permanently signed into accounts is not advised. Regular users of unencrypted websites are encouraged to use a virtual private network (VPN), which can encrypt the data moving between your computer and the Internet. VPNs are especially useful because they can encrypt data flowing even on an unsecured network. Even users of encrypted Wi-Fi hotspots are cautioned that all encryptions are not of equal strength. Some may be more susceptible to hacking.[20]

In addition, other commonsense precautions should be taken, such as keeping an up-to-date antivirus program on your computer, refraining from sending especially sensitive private information such as financial information whenever possible, and heeding warnings about possibly infected programs or files. Physical control of your computer should be maintained at all times. Never leave a computer unattended even for a brief time. It takes only seconds for a thief to steal a computer. While the loss of your computer may be personally upsetting, those working on employer-owned computers may be risking not only their own personal information but also personally identifiable information belonging to others. Most of us have heard or read about privacy breaches that have resulted from an employee's inattention. Laptops containing personally identifiable information have been stolen or lost. Others have been hacked. We must always remember that we are responsible for taking actions to ensure privacy protection. We cannot assume that this is the responsibility of others and that the companies that we do business with online have taken all the necessary actions to ensure information privacy.

Spying and Webcam Safety

Users should also be cautioned about the vulnerabilities of cameras or webcams on the computers they are using. It might be possible for others to spy on them through the webcams. The FTC has reported on an egregious spying practice that, through the use of software, can allow the activation of a webcam without the computer user's knowledge. According to the FTC, the software company, DesignerWare, provided software to Aaron's Inc., known to many as Aaron's Rent-to-Own, that allowed the rent-to-own company to "take screenshots of confidential and personal information, log customers' computer keystrokes and, in some cases, to take webcam pictures of people in their own homes, all without the customers' knowledge."[21] Finding this practice to be deceptive, the FTC prohibited Aaron's Inc. from further using the monitoring technology, and required them to get the consent of consumers before using location-tracking software.[22] In an April 2013 press release the FTC reported that "the software company, DesignerWare, and its principals . . . will be barred from providing others with the means to commit illegal acts."[23] While this is good news, it raises concerns about how many others may have the power to activate webcams without the knowledge of users.

DesignerWare may not be alone in its ability to spy on users and activate webcams. The *Washington Post*[24] and the UK's *Daily Mail Online*[25] have both recently reported on the FBI's ability to spy on individuals using webcams. According to a December 6, 2013, article in the *Washington Post*, the FBI has apparently created and is able to secretly deliver malicious software that can "covertly download files, photographs and stored e-mails, or even gather real-time images by activating cameras connected to computers."[26] The *Daily Mail Online* also reports that there has been an increase in the use of "remote administration tools" to hack into the webcams of unsuspecting women and spy on them.[27] This means that it is a good idea to cover your webcam lens when you are not using it. While an up-to-date antivirus program may find many viruses, it may not be able to keep all prying away from your webcam.

Adjusting Browser Privacy and Security Settings

Information professionals should advise those who use Internet Explorer to surf the web that it is a good idea to use the InPrivate browsing feature whenever possible. This feature, according to Microsoft, allows you to surf the web "but things like passwords, search history, and webpage history are deleted when you close the browser." Another important feature is "Do Not Track." This is an option under the advanced security settings. While it will not stop all tracking, it can help limit tracking by sending a message to websites that users do not want to be tracked. Another possible privacy protection that is offered by Microsoft is "Tracking Protection." When using tracking protection a user would install a "Tracking Protection List" that Microsoft likens to a "do not call" list. Internet Explorer then "blocks third-party content from sites on the list" and limits what information they can collect.[28]

Those searching the Internet using Mozilla Firefox can do several things to increase the level of privacy they enjoy while on the web. Under the privacy settings in Mozilla Firefox, a user can select "Tell sites that I do not want to be tracked." A user can also select "Always use private browsing mode" and refuse to accept third party cookies or limit them to sites that the user has visited.[29] In the security settings of Mozilla Firefox, a user can also elect to be warned when sites try to install add-ons, block reported attack sites, and block reported web forgeries.[30] A good practice for web surfing generally is to regularly clear your search history. This is especially important if the user is accessing the Internet on a public computer. The next person who uses the computer can access your history, which may include information you wish to keep private.

Privacy and security settings can be increased on other web browsers as well. As libraries generally control these settings for their stationary computers, it may not be an issue for them, but it is still advisable for them to share this information with patron Wi-Fi users. Youth should be advised to monitor their privacy and safety settings. Employees should receive education in this as well for those using laptops. Security departments may wish to contribute to employee education and participate in joint or integrated training sessions.

MOBILE DEVICES AND INFORMATION PRIVACY

It is no secret that by agreeing to the terms of use of many mobile apps, users forfeit aspects of their privacy. Our smart phones can be used to track where we go and what we do and to disclose patterns of our daily lives. Our personal information may be used in ways we had not considered. Sometimes the forfeitures of our privacy seem extreme when we hear horror stories of notices for applications (apps) that include the unnecessary ability of an app provider to copy contact lists or have the ability to turn a phone on and record information.[31] Many of us, however, may not be aware of some of the perils of our selection of mobile device. A December 14, 2013, article in *InformationWeek* highlights the control that mobile-device makers have. The article reports on a feature that, according to Thomas Claburn, was removed from Google's Android phones. The feature was an "undocumented App Ops control panel" that allowed savvy users to choose which app permissions to enable. This meant that users could deny permissions for location tracking. [32]

Google is not alone in limiting choices when it comes to apps. Anyone with an Apple iPhone knows that in the app world, for now at least, a user must accept all terms or forgo getting the app. While the FTC offers sensible advice to app creators on its website and encourages them to build privacy considerations in from the start, stronger protections are still needed. [33] Users need to read the privacy policies and opt-out if they are unfair. It is only through such actions that change will occur concerning our privacy in the app world.

Owners of mobile devices such as phones, tablets, and so on must remember to password protect these devices to help ensure privacy. Once lost or stolen they may be windows into our social lives and personal information. An unsecured device may allow direct access not only to our personal information but also to online sites such as Facebook accounts and webmail. Reports of mobile phone thieves posting pictures to Facebook accounts are growing.[34] Mobile device users should also investigate mobile apps that are capable of finding your device and wiping the data from it, and in the case of a mobile phone, some are capable of contacting your phone and displaying a custom message and contact number on the locked screen. Taking actions to protect your personal information in the event that your phone is stolen can offer some piece of mind.

KEEP ABREAST OF CHANGES

One of the biggest challenges in protecting our information privacy and the information privacy of others is keeping abreast of changes in the law, technology, and aspects of our respective work environments that can affect privacy. Investigating news services devoted to privacy, technology, security, and trade news can help us stay informed. Scanning news sites for the latest privacy-focused information, joining online privacy groups, subscribing to alerts, reviewing privacy blogs, reading some of the recently published privacy books, and regularly reviewing sites such as the FTC's website assist in privacy awareness.

THE PROMISE OF SAFER WEB SURFING

In response to the news of widespread NSA surveillance, more focus has been placed on increasing online privacy. A number of options for more private web surfing have emerged. Google launched an encrypted search option in May of 2010. It is accessible at https://encrypted.google.com. [35] Another search option that promises to collect and share absolutely no data about users is Startpage by ixquick. It is accessible at https://startpage.com/eng. Startpage's motto is "the world's most *private* search engine." Startpage, a Dutch company, offers searching "enhanced by Google." Another search engine offering enhanced privacy is Duck Duck Go, https://duckduckgo.com. Duck Duck Go also offers educational information about how your information is collected online and used. Investigating and incorporating educational sessions about the availability and benefits of encrypted sites and those that do not collect or forward user information is recommended for those providing guidance to users of all ages and backgrounds.

CONCLUSION

Educating patrons, youth, and employees about the privacy perils of Internet use is necessary to help ensure that their private information and that held by their employers remains secure. While information breaches do occur, many can be avoided with thorough and continuing information privacy and security education. Those working in libraries, schools, and other areas where shared computers are in use are advised to post notices near computers that inform users about the dangers of personal information being gathered and the many ways it may be gathered online. Initial and continuing privacy and security training is recommended for all groups of users. Technology continues to change and online users must keep abreast of privacy vulnerabilities.

Information professionals should continue their own educations in these areas to make sure that they can provide up-to-date training and assistance.

Ultimately, in this age of extensive data mining, marketing, and diminished privacy controls, users must take responsibility for ensuring their own private information. Careful consideration must be given to the sharing of information online, to the privacy policies we agree to, and to where and how we make use of what the Internet has to offer. Remaining mindful of our physical surroundings, our privacy settings, and the many ways that our personal information can be obtained and used is the key to safeguarding our own private information and the private information of others. While most information professionals may be aware and know how to secure their own personal information, it is important to always remember that those around us may not have had the same training. Incorporating information privacy education into digital and information training will help to ensure that what we wish to keep private individually, professionally, and in the workplace will remain private.

NOTES

1. A June 24, 2011, editorial in the *Toronto Star* quotes Canada's privacy commissioner, Jennifer Stoddard, stating that "the public needs to be imbued with more 'privacy literacy.'" Dana Rotman also uses the term in a poster presentation in 2009 advocating for a "privacy literacy framework" and situating privacy literacy as a "sub-category of digital literacy, or . . . a complementing literacy." D. Rotman, "Are You Looking at Me? Social Media and Privacy Literacy." Poster presented at the 2009 iConference, February 8–11, 2009, Chapel Hill, NC, available   online   at   www.ideals.illinois.edu/bitstream/handle/2142/15339/ Are_You_Looking_at_Me_-_Social_Media_And_Privacy_Literacy_-_final.pdf?sequence=2.

2. ALA Digital Technology Taskforce, "What Is Digital Literacy?," ALA Office of Information   Technology   Policy,   2011,   http://connect.ala.org/files/94226/ what%20is%20digilit%20%282%29.pdf.

3. Ibid.

4. "Information Literacy Competency Standards for Higher Education," Association of College & Research Libraries, www.ala.org/acrl/standards/informationliteracycompetency#f1 (accessed December 8, 2013).

5. Jeannette Woodward, *What Every Librarian Should Know about Electronic Privacy* (Westport CT: Libraries Unlimited, 2007), 2–9.

6. "Information and Privacy Commissioner of Ontario Ann Cavoukian, PhD," YouTube, www.youtube.com/watch?v=IiEvRZzQnHM (accessed December 13, 2013).

7. Many different sources are available online. Several sources from Canada are particularly recommended including the following: Media Smarts Canada's Centre for Digital and Media Literacy, "Privacy Pirates: An Interactive Unit on Online Privacy (Ages 7–9)," http://mediasmarts.ca/game/privacy-pirates-interactive-unit-online-privacy-ages-7-9 (accessed March 9, 2014); Office of the Privacy Commissioner of Canada, "Social Smarts: Privacy, the Internet, and You," www.priv.gc.ca/youth-jeunes/fs-fi/res/gn_e.pdf (accessed March 9, 2014).

8. Adobe's Flash plug-in is free software for viewing multimedia. "What Are Local Shared Objects?," Adobe, April 6, 2014, www.adobe.com/security/flashplayer/articles/lso.

9. "Manage Cookies," All About Cookies, April 6, 2014, www.allaboutcookies.org/manage-cookies/remove-flash-cookies.html.

10. "What Are Web Beacons and How Do They Generate SPAM?," Microsoft Support, http://office.microsoft.com/en-us/outlook-help/what-are-web-beacons-and-how-do-they-generate-more-spam-HA010271019.aspx (accessed December 15, 2013).

11. "Web Beacons," Yahoo, http://info.yahoo.com/privacy/us/yahoo/webbeacons (accessed December 15, 2013).

12. Associate information with a person or entity. Data miners are able to analyze certain information from databases, which on their own provide anonymous data, to identify data with specific individuals.

13. Electronic Privacy Information Center, "Re-Identification: Concerning the Re-Identification of Consumer Information," epic.org, http://epic.org/privacy/reidentification/#intro (accessed December 15, 2013).

14. Search logs: Search logs are exactly what they sound like. They are a listing of search requests that show what search queries you typed into the Internet. They are tied to IP addresses. Companies such as Google save these logs and use them for data mining, and examination by law enforcement and government agencies.

15. Director Cullen Hoback, "Terms and Conditions May Apply," Demand Progress, www.demandprogress.tv (accessed November 17, 2013).

16. Caitlin Dewey, "The NSA Might Be Reading Your Searches, but Your Local Police Probably Aren't," *Washington Post*, August 3, 2013, available online at www.washingtonpost.com/blogs/the-switch/wp/2013/08/03/the-nsa-might-be-reading-your-searches-but-your-local-police-probably-arent.

17. Amy Mitchell and Emily Guskin, "Twitter News Consumers: Young, Mobile and Educated," PEW Research Journalism Project, November 4, 2013, www.journalism.org/2013/11/04/twitter-news-consumers-young-mobile-and-educated.

18. "Library of Congress Is Archiving All of America's Tweets," *Business Insider*, January 22, 2103, available online at www.businessinsider.com/library-of-congress-is-archiving-all-of-americas-tweets-2013-1#ixzz2nJ2koztM.

19. ActiveX is a small software component of Microsoft Windows that controls add-ins from websites. For more on ActiveX, see Microsoft's explanation available at www.microsoft.com/security/resources/activex-whatis.aspx (accessed May 7, 2014).

20. "Tips for Using Public Wi-Fi Networks," OnGuardOnline.gov, Federal Trade Commission, www.onguardonline.gov/articles/0014-tips-using-public-wi-fi-networks (accessed December 13, 2013).

21. "FTC Approves Final Order Settling Charges Against Software and Rent-to-Own Companies Accused of Computer Spying," Federal Trade Commission, April 15, 2013, www.ftc.gov/news-events/press-releases/2013/04/ftc-approves-final-order-settling-charges-against-software-and.

22. "Aaron's Rent-to-Own Chain Settles FTC Charges That It Enabled Computer Spying by Franchisees," Federal Trade Commission, October 22, 2013, www.ftc.gov/news-events/press-releases/2013/10/aarons-rent-own-chain-settles-ftc-charges-it-enabled-computer.

23. "FTC Approves Final Order."

24. Craig Timberg and Ellen Nakashima, "FBI's Search for 'Mo,' Suspect in Bomb Threats, Highlights Use of Malware for Surveillance," *Washington Post*, December 6, 2013, available online at www.washingtonpost.com/business/technology/fbis-search-for-mo-suspect-in-bomb-threats-highlights-use-of-malware-for-surveillance/2013/12/06/352ba174-5397-11e3-9e2c-e1d01116fd98_story.html.

25. Sara Malm, "FBI Can Spy on You through Your Webcam Without Triggering the Indicator Light . . . and Has Had the Technology for Several Years," Mail Online, December 9, 2013, www.dailymail.co.uk/news/article-2520707/FBI-spy-webcam-triggering-indicator-light.html#ixzz2nVMbpu9A.

26. Timberg and Nakashima, " FBI's Search for 'Mo.'"

27. Malm, "FBI Can Spy on You."

28. "Helping Protect Your Privacy," Microsoft Windows, http://windows.microsoft.com/en-us/windows-8/browse-web-internet-explorer-tutorial (accessed December 10, 2013).

29. "Privacy Settings," Mozilla Firefox start page (accessed December 10, 2013).

30. "Security Settings," Mozilla Firefox start page (accessed December 10, 2013).

31. Both of these scenarios were raised at a continuing privacy education session in 2013.

32. Thomas Claburn, "Google Yanks Buried Android Privacy Feature," *InformationWeek*, December 14, 2013, www.informationweek.com/mobile/mobile-business/google-yanks-buried-android-privacy-feature/d/d-id/1113093?f_src=informationweek_gnews.

33. "Marketing Your Mobile App: Get It Right from the Start," Bureau of Consumer Protection Business Center, Federal Trade Commission, April 2013, www.business.ftc.gov/documents/bus81-marketing-your-mobile-app.

34. Zahid Arab, "iPhone Thief Posts Picture on Victim's Facebook Page," King5.com, August 4, 2013, updated August 5, 2013, www.king5.com/news/cities/bremerton/After-iPhone-thief-posts-photo-Facebook-218306291.html; Philip Caulfield, "Pickpocket Victim Stunned to Find Intimate Pics of iPhone Thief's Family, Pregnant Belly," New York Daily News, January 7, 2014, www.nydailynews.com/news/national/victim-stunned-pics-iphone-thief-family-pregnant-belly-article-1.1568812; Mark Hattersley, " iPhone Thief Accidentally Posts His Photo to Victim's Facebook," *IT World*, March 18, 2013, www.itworld.com/348685/pot-smoking-iphone-thief-accidentally-posts-his-photo-victims-facebook.

35. More information about the encrypted Google site and the history of its updates are available on Google's official blog at http://googleblog.blogspot.com/2010/05/search-more-securely-with-encrypted.html.

BIBLIOGRAPHY

American Library Association. "Presidential Committee on Information Literacy. Final Report." Association of College & Research Libraries, January 10, 1989. www.ala.org/acrl/publications/whitepapers/presidential.

American Library Association Digital Technology Taskforce. "What Is Digital Literacy?" ALA Office of Information Technology Policy, 2011. http://connect.ala.org/files/94226/what%20is%20digilit%20%282%29.pdf.

Claburn, Thomas. "Google Yanks Buried Android Privacy Feature." InformationWeek, December 14, 2013. www.informationweek.com/mobile/mobile-business/google-yanks-buried-android-privacy-feature/d/d-id/1113093?f_src=informationweek_gnews.

Dewey, Caitlin. "The NSA Might Be Reading Your Searches, but Your Local Police Probably Aren't." *Washington Post*, August 3, 2013. www.washingtonpost.com/blogs/the-switch/wp/2013/08/03/the-nsa-might-be-reading-your-searches-but-your-local-police-probably-arent.

Electronic Privacy Information Center. "Re-Identification: Concerning the Re-Identification of Consumer Information." epic.org. http://epic.org/privacy/reidentification/#intro (accessed December 15, 2013).

Horowitz, Michael. "What Does Your IP Address Say about You?" CNET, September 15, 2008. http://news.cnet.com/8301-13554_3-10042206-33.html.

"Information Literacy Competency Standards for Higher Education." Association of College & Research Libraries. www.ala.org/acrl/standards/informationliteracycompetency#f1 (accessed December 8, 2013).

"Library of Congress is Archiving All of America's Tweets." *Business Insider*, January 22, 2103. Available online at www.businessinsider.com/library-of-congress-is-archiving-all-of-americas-tweets-2013-1#ixzz2nJ2koztM.

Malm, Sara. "FBI Can Spy on You through Your Webcam Without Triggering the Indicator Light . . . and Has Had the Technology for Several Years." Mail Online, December 9, 2013. www.dailymail.co.uk/news/article-2520707/FBI-spy-webcam-triggering-indicator-light.html#ixzz2nVMbpu9A.

"Marketing Your Mobile App: Get It Right from the Start." Bureau of Consumer Protection Business Center, Federal Trade Commission, April 2013. www.business.ftc.gov/documents/bus81-marketing-your-mobile-app.

Mitchell, Amy, and Emily Guskin. "Twitter News Consumers: Young, Mobile and Educated." PEW Research Journalism Project, November 4, 2013. www.journalism.org/2013/11/04/twitter-news-consumers-young-mobile-and-educated/.

Timberg, Craig, and Ellen Nakashima. "FBI's Search for 'Mo,' Suspect in Bomb Threats, Highlights Use of Malware for Surveillance." *Washington Post*, December 6, 2013. Available online at www.washingtonpost.com/business/technology/fbis-search-for-mo-suspect-in-bomb-threats-highlights-use-of-malware-for-surveillance/2013/12/06/352ba174-5397-11e3-9e2c-e1d01116fd98_story.html.

Woodward, Jeannette. *What Every Librarian Should Know about Electronic Privacy*. Westport, CT: Libraries Unlimited, 2007.

Chapter Five

Information Privacy in Libraries

Not surprisingly, public concern about information privacy continues to grow. During the past 15 years, we have witnessed an increase in data mining, an increase in hacking and spying efforts, and reports of data breaches (primarily due to laws requiring companies to report these breaches). The understanding that our online searching and buying habits are tracked and that this information is amassed and mined is becoming more commonplace. As discussed in chapter 4, there are things that users can and should do to deter data tracking and data collection efforts online.

The public library serves as one of the few remaining venues where individuals feel free to explore and receive information with some expectation of anonymity. However, as noted earlier, the perceived value of Internet access provided by the library may decline if the privacy of anonymity is not protected and maintained.

This chapter focuses on the value of privacy in the library, key privacy concerns, and some ways that libraries can mitigate those concerns. The importance of protecting privacy in libraries has been addressed in chapter 2. This discussion builds on those principles and arguments and provides issues to consider when creating library privacy policies and notices.

GREATER ANONYMITY

In many libraries, even if patrons are required to sign in to use the Internet, their information is held by the library, usually for a limited time, and not made available to others unless the library is required to do so by law. This provides a level of anonymity when searching online because the information search on the library's computers is not automatically tied to the patron who performed it. While such anonymity may be compromised by personal information divulged online, such as personal passwords and other identifying information, it is more difficult to identify patrons using library computers and the library IP address than those using personal computers.

The benefit of more anonymous searching was made clear by a reported incident involving the retailer Target. In February 2012, the *New York Times* ran an article about how companies predict and influence our shopping habits and highlighted efforts of Target to get us to buy more goods.

Through the use of data mining and analysis of online activity, Target was able to predict with some accuracy which shoppers were pregnant based on their purchases and then send them coupons to increase their purchases. In one such case, the company targeted a high school student with printed coupons that brought a complaint by her father. A follow-up phone call to the young woman's father showed that Target was correct that the young woman was pregnant. She simply hadn't shared this information yet with her father. Through data mining and advertising, Target made public the private information that this young woman had not yet chosen to share. It is a chilling thought that some of the information that we wish to keep private can so easily be exposed by companies seeking to snare us into buying more from them.[1] The relative anonymity of library computers offers patrons a buffer from some efforts to mine their information.

PROTECTING PRIVACY AND CONFIDENTIALITY ON THE FRONT LINES

Librarians and other library staff are on the front lines of privacy protection. They are the ones most likely to field questions about patron information, but are they prepared? Do they know and understand the applicable privacy laws? Do directors believe that their staffs know how to implement library policies and procedures concerning patron privacy and confidentiality?

One researcher, Trina Magi, set out to investigate how many public and academic libraries in the state of Vermont take specific measures to protect patron confidentiality beyond having a written policy. She also sought to determine how confident directors were in their own abilities and the abilities of their staffs to follow confidentiality policies. The results are interesting.

The findings of Trina Magi's 2006 survey of public and academic library directors in Vermont indicate that while a majority of library directors felt that they could carry out their library's confidentiality policy, they were less confident about the abilities of staff and were concerned about the need to educate volunteers.[2] Responses also indicate a desire by the directors for assistance "developing/writing library confidentiality policy or procedures."[3] Of course, there is more that can be done to move beyond general policies and create specific procedures accompanied by training for all library staff, volunteers, and library users.

Procedures are needed to advise new library technicians and other support staff about what to do when faced with information requests from individuals or entities other than the patron. Student workers and volunteers need training to understand how to address privacy issues and how to increase privacy and the perception of privacy in libraries. It is time to move from the ideal to the applied.

Indeed, Magi's study reveals some practices in public libraries that compromise patron privacy such as phone messages that identify the name of the patron and the items either available for pick-up or overdue for return.[4] Other practices that compromise patrons' privacy include placing patrons' names on hold materials that are visible to the public and placing holds in a common area for patron pick-up. Both actions make it possible to match materials with specific patrons. While it is understood that there is a balancing of patron privacy with efforts to save on costs and improve accessibility, such actions raise privacy concerns that should be carefully examined.

Do these practices limit patron inquiry? Are some patrons simply not going to request books on sensitive topics because of these practices? Could others use the information gleaned from looking at the holds to embarrass or otherwise harm the requesting patrons? Careful thought must be given to all actions in the library and their impact on patron privacy and confidentiality.

Privacy must be made a priority so that time is dedicated to privacy training for staff, to the creation of privacy policies and procedures, and to privacy risk assessments. In order to be successful, an environment must be created where privacy is given a high importance by all, especially those in management and executive positions. They can set priorities for investment of resources and set the tone for the library and its branches.

PATRON AWARENESS

In this time of increasing concern about our individual privacy rights, libraries should publicize the privacy protections they offer and make their limitations known to users in plain English and at levels appropriate for all to understand. Not only is it an important public relations tool, but it can also help to increase privacy awareness and privacy literacy. Businesses publicize privacy policies so that customers know how their data will be used, including whether that information can be made available to a third party or affiliate.

Visible privacy policies can provide patrons with information about how their information may be used. Notices about what the library is doing to protect patron privacy can go a long to way to educating patrons and instilling a sense of trust not only about each patron's relationship with the library but also about every patron's ability to explore their intellectual curiosity without worry about public scrutiny.

A shorter notice is recommended with links to a longer privacy policy when the policy is too long to quickly and easily convey a clear message about what the library is doing to protect patron privacy. The notice with links to the full policy can be placed on library computers as part of an initial homepage screen for patrons to review. Shorter notices with information about where to view the full policy can also be placed in strategic locations within the library. Library privacy policies can address and inform patrons about specific concerns about applicable laws, collection techniques, and technology that is or may be used in the library.

THE USA PATRIOT ACT

The Uniting and Strengthening America by Providing Appropriate Tools Required to Intercept and Obstruct Terrorism, or USA PATRIOT Act, was introduced and passed in 2001. It has been a significant cause for concern among library privacy advocates. Provisions of the Act due to expire were renewed for an additional four years in 2011.

In the wake of recent NSA revelations about widespread domestic information gathering, concern has increased about clandestine data collection, and how the PATRIOT Act may be being used to authorize the collection of data on individuals in the United States. The specter of secret surveillance and concern about who is mining our personal data and how they are determining possible national security threats has created a feeling of unease among many privacy advocates. Even American writers have acknowledged concern about this type of secret information gathering and use.[5] A study conducted on behalf of PEN America found that writers are self-censoring, fearing that researching, writing, or commenting on certain topics "will cause them harm."[6] In this environment, it is more important than ever to demonstrate how libraries are protecting information privacy so that patrons of all ages can feel free to exercise their intellectual curiosity.

MINIMIZING DATA COLLECTION AND RETENTION

Data Collection

Libraries can help protect privacy by reviewing all data-collection practices and uses to determine if the collection of personal information is necessary. Could these functions or services be accomplished with less data or without personal identifiers? Unless the collection and retention of personal information is needed to perform necessary functions or services, libraries should make it a priority to cease or reduce these activities. Reducing the collection and use of personal data provides users with a greater level of control concerning their information privacy. If personal data must be collected, the collection of this data and the ways it is and can be put to use should be clearly explained in the privacy policy. Notice should also be given when users access services so that they can make informed decisions.

Observability

The need for privacy to be able to express intellectual curiosity is not isolated to computer and circulation records. Thought should be given to the impact of security cameras that point to sections of the library. While these cameras may be necessary, consideration should be given to how long those recordings are held, who has access to them, and how they are used. In the same vein, the placement of computers or the option of installing privacy screens is another avenue for increasing privacy and reducing concerns about observability.

The placement of sensitive reading materials can also impact whether patrons, especially teens, feel free to explore library materials. The actions of library staff and the placement of staff in the library can also have an effect on intellectual exploration. Adults and teens may be hesitant to seek information about sensitive topics if the placement of those materials is in view of library staff, highly trafficked areas, or where they may be recorded by cameras or otherwise identified while viewing materials. If patrons wish to review materials without fear of public or staff scrutiny, the placement of those materials must be considered as part of the overall patron privacy in libraries.

RFID SYSTEMS IN LIBRARIES

The use of radio frequency identification (RFID) technology in libraries in recent years has also caused privacy concerns. As more libraries adopt this technology and the advances in this technology continue to grow, library professionals should consider what information could be stored on RFID chips, whether someone other than the library staff could access the information stored on RFID chips placed in library materials, and whether this information could be intercepted and linked to other records.[7]

The ALA's Office of Intellectual Freedom (OIF) has provided policy guidelines for implementing RFID technology[8] and recommends educating library patrons about the use of this technology and, where possible, offering an "'opt-in' system" so that patrons can choose whether they want to borrow materials using this technology.[9] In addition to this information, the OIF's recommendations generally follow those of other privacy guidelines concerning the use of RFID technology.

Both the OIF and the former Information and Privacy Commissioner of Ontario, Ann Cavoukian, offer guidance concerning "best practices" that will serve libraries well as they consider how to protect patron privacy when using RFID technology.[10] Cavoukian's guidelines highlight the danger of tracking and surveillance through the use of RFID technology.[11] She urges entities to consider the use of RFID at the system level and to build in privacy and security protections from the beginning.[12] This is especially helpful for those libraries considering the use of RFID technology. An assessment of the privacy and security risks involved in adopting RFID technology in a library or library system must be done prior to implementation. This type of assessment, known as a privacy impact assessment, can help minimize the risks of patron identification and tracking.

Privacy notices should contain information about the use of RFID in the library and identify if there is a means to elect not to use this technology. The notice should also explain what information is collected and used by the RFID system, the retention and disclosure practices, how individuals can access this information, and information about the auditing process of this technology. When possible, efforts should be made to ensure that no personal information is recorded on RFID chips and that security measures are in place to prevent outside linkage to patron records.

LEARNING FROM PRIVACY PRACTICES OF SMALL AND MEDIUM-SIZED BUSINESSES

Libraries need not start from scratch to decide how best to keep private and secure the personal information of patrons, including names, addresses, phone numbers, email addresses, dates of birth, records of books checked out, search logs from computer use, and in some cases records of databases accessed. They can look for guidance in the practices of small and medium-sized businesses that must adhere to federal and state privacy laws and implement measures to safeguard the personal information of their customers. Libraries can reproduce private sector privacy education programs for library patrons and training for employees, volunteers, and anyone else working on behalf of the library.

Libraries can also implement Privacy by Design (PbD).[13] PbD is a new approach to privacy that incorporates privacy concerns into all aspects of design. Ann Cavoukian developed this concept, which is being used in government and industry. It starts with putting privacy considerations at the forefront of technology and project designs as well as business practices. Employing PbD enables organizations to take a more thoughtful and comprehensive approach to protecting information privacy. It focuses on transparency and on the user. Using PbD in libraries would help to ensure the protection of personal information at all stages by keeping it a priority and would highlight the focus on patrons' rights. PbD requires that privacy be a part of any information-technology changes, management considerations, and regular education.

Libraries can and should examine how they are collecting and using personal information. They should determine how they can limit what they collect. Workflows and who has access to private information should be carefully scrutinized. The fewer employees and third parties accessing personal data, the safer it will be. Employing the use of privacy assessments used in industry and government agencies can assist in this endeavor.

THE ROLE OF PRIVACY PROFESSIONALS

Information privacy is about balancing the needs of privacy with those of access while adhering to applicable laws. Privacy professionals and others working in privacy must understand privacy concerns, laws and regulations, as well as best practices and how to implement them. Privacy policies are needed to guide action and to guide what types of security measures are used. Remember security exists in more than the digital world. Policies help to iron out the competing interests and adhere to law.

If we were to approach information privacy strictly from a security point of view, we could lock up the information and make it inaccessible. However, sensible information privacy needs more than an understanding of security and privacy laws. There must be a reasonable balancing of the need to use information and the obligation to keep it secure. Privacy professionals work with specialists in information technology and security to create policies to address how security is implemented and to facilitate access to personal information as needed to perform business activities. In a library setting the same principles apply.

Libraries can model the actions of businesses and government agencies by appointing someone on staff to keep abreast of privacy. This individual would work with the director and others to create and revise privacy policies and procedures and to examine any changes that have occurred in library programming, services, systems, and all other aspects of the library. The privacy professional would be responsible for coordinating and implementing of all of the library's privacy and confidentiality efforts.

Appointing someone to manage library privacy will help the library to reach its goals of increasing patron privacy and complying with applicable privacy laws. This individual can lead privacy initiatives and guide others. He or she can serve as a source of information and advice in the workplace and promote privacy and the message of its importance to the library board, the general public, patrons, and staff.

Having a dedicated privacy professional means that there will be a dedicated person to seek input from the legal department and assist in obtaining approval of policies and procedures. A privacy professional can also provide a strong foundation for supporting the library when incidents arise and privacy is challenged.

LOCATING AND EXAMINING PRIVACY LAWS

Libraries should examine federal and state laws addressing privacy as they consider what privacy measures are needed and what information to include in privacy policies and notices. Federal laws and how to find them are addressed in chapter 3 of this book. Libraries also can look to state attorneys general for guidance on privacy regulation in their own states.

Each state's attorney general has a website and this is generally where privacy laws will be found. The National Conference of State Legislatures (NCSL) also provides information about Internet privacy laws by state and is updated regularly.[14] This site includes information about children's online privacy, e-reader privacy, privacy policies for websites, state laws addressing personal information held by ISPs, and more. The NCSL also provides a listing of the states that include privacy protection in their state constitutions along with the texts of those laws.[15] In short, there are many online sites to assist in identifying applicable privacy laws, creating privacy policies, and implementing and best practices. It is time for those in library and information science to seek additional guidance from outside the field.

DEDICATING TIME FOR PRIVACY REVIEW AND TRAINING

Those in the privacy community celebrate Data Privacy Day. This is an action that libraries should emulate. They could dedicate that day to providing training for employees, providing educational opportunities for patrons, and making privacy a priority. Coordinating reviews of privacy measures on that day could be helpful. While reviews of the status of privacy measures and new options in privacy and security should be performed more regularly, dedicating Data Privacy Day to include reexamining current privacy and security practices and providing training and education is an excellent way to keep privacy a priority.

CONCLUSION

In order to provide information privacy in library settings, the staff of each library must have a clear understanding of the federal and state laws protecting or impacting privacy in their libraries and within any parent institutions. It is important to remember that managing information privacy is a form of information management. When practicing information privacy, we are analyzing privacy issues surrounding information and making decisions about how to manage information to ensure privacy. This is why privacy and security training for employees is essential.

Providing privacy notices and privacy literacy education to those who use the library also works to ensure privacy. Educating employees, patrons, students, and the general public about how to properly manage personally identifiable information to ensure their own privacy and the privacy of others is needed in libraries and in other institutions across the globe. Ignorance of privacy issues means that libraries and other entities are more susceptible to privacy and security breaches. Comprehensive privacy policies, procedures, and checklists are needed to help ensure patron and staff privacy. These policies should be reviewed by legal counsel to determine that they comply with all applicable federal and state laws. It is recommended that procedures also be examined to get approval for specific responses when addressing law enforcement and other requests for information.

This chapter has offered a broad look at key privacy issues in libraries and models for libraries to emulate. It offered a new vision of the role of privacy professionals in libraries. More specific examination of what should be included in privacy policies and notices for libraries will be addressed in chapter 6.

NOTES

1. Charles, Duhigg, "How Companies Learn Your Secrets," *New York Times*, February 16, 2012, available online at www.nytimes.com/2012/02/19/magazine/shopping-habits.html?pagewanted=5&_r=1&hp.

2. Trina Magi, "A Study of US Library Directors Confidence and Practice Regarding Patron Confidentiality," *Library Management* 29, no. 8/9 (2008): 746–56. Magi's survey was sent to all 213 directors of public and academic libraries in Vermont. She received a 75 percent response rate.

3. Ibid., 750.

4. Ibid., 750–51.

5. The FDR Group, "Chilling Effects: NSA Surveillance Drives U.S. Writers to Self-Censor," Pen America, November 12, 2013, www.pen.org/sites/default/files/Chilling%20Effects_PEN%20American.pdf, 6.

6. The FDR Group, "Chilling Effects," 6. According to the report, the survey was completed by "528 PEN members" ("Methodology").

7. "Radio Frequency Identification (RFID) Systems," EPIC, http://epic.org/privacy/rfid (accessed February 2, 2014). NISO RFID Revision Working Group, *RFID in Libraries: A*

Recommended Practice of the National Information Standards Organization (Baltimore: National Information Standards Organization, 2012), available online at www.niso.org/apps/group_public/download.php/8269/RP-6-2012_RFID-in_US_Libraries.pdf.

8. Office of Intellectual Freedom, comp, *Intellectual Freedom Manual*, 8th ed. (Chicago: American Library Association, 2010).

9. Ibid., 285.

10. Ann Cavoukian, "Privacy Guidelines for RFID Information Systems," Information and Privacy Commissioner, Ontario, Canada, June 2006, www.ipc.on.ca/images/Resources/up-rfidgdlines.pdf.

11. Ibid., 1.

12. Ibid., 2.

13. Ann Cavoukian, "Operationalizing Privacy by Design: A Guide to Implementing Strong Privacy Practices," Information and Privacy Commissioner, Ontario, Canada, December 2012, www.privacybydesign.ca/content/uploads/2013/01/operationalizing-pbd-guide.pdf.

14. "State Laws Related to Internet Privacy," National Conference of State Legislatures, updated January 24, 2014, www.ncsl.org/research/telecommunications-and-information-technology/state-laws-related-to-internet-privacy.aspx (accessed February 2, 2014).

15. "Privacy Protections in State Constitutions," National Conference of State Legislatures, updated December 11, 2013, www.ncsl.org/research/telecommunications-and-information-technology/privacy-protections-in-state-constitutions.aspx (accessed February 2, 2014).

BIBLIOGRAPHY

Cavoukian, Ann. "Operationalizing Privacy by Design: A Guide to Implementing Strong Privacy Practices." Information and Privacy Commissioner, Ontario, Canada, December 2012. www.privacybydesign.ca/content/uploads/2013/01/operationalizing-pbd-guide.pdf.

———. "Privacy Guidelines for RFID Information Systems." Information and Privacy Commissioner, Ontario, Canada, June 2006. www.ipc.on.ca/images/Resources/up-rfidg-dlines.pdf.

Duhigg, Charles. "How Companies Learn Your Secrets." *New York Times*, February 16, 2012. Available online at www.nytimes.com/2012/02/19/magazine/shopping-habits.html?pagewanted=5&_r=1&hp.

The FDR Group. "Chilling Effects: NSA Surveillance Drives U.S. Writers to Self-Censor." Pen America, November 12, 2013. www.pen.org/sites/default/files/Chilling%20Effects_PEN%20American.pdf.

Magi, Trina. "A Study of US Library Directors Confidence and Practice Regarding Patron Confidentiality." *Library Management* 29, no. 8/9 (2008): 746–56.

NISO RFID Revision Working Group. *RFID in Libraries: A Recommended Practice of the National Information Standards Organization.* Baltimore: National Information Standards Organization, 2012. Available online at www.niso.org/apps/group_public/download.php/8269/RP-6-2012_RFID-in_US_Libraries.pdf.

Office of Intellectual Freedom, comp. *Intellectual Freedom Manual.* 8th edition. Chicago: American Library Association, 2010.

"Privacy Protections in State Constitutions." National Conference of State Legislatures, updated December 11, 2013. www.ncsl.org/research/telecommunications-and-information-technology/privacy-protections-in-state-constitutions.aspx (accessed February 2, 2014).

"Radio Frequency Identification (RFID) Systems." EPIC. http://epic.org/privacy/rfid (accessed February 2, 2014).

"State Laws Related to Internet Privacy." National Conference of State Legislatures, updated January 24, 2014. www.ncsl.org/research/telecommunications-and-information-technology/state-laws-related-to-internet-privacy.aspx (accessed February 2, 2014).

Chapter Six

Privacy Policies and Programs

Understanding information privacy issues, and the laws applicable to them, provides the foundation necessary to begin developing information privacy policies. However, at the time of this writing, there is a shortage of information professionals with this training. The ability to understand privacy law, the role of information privacy, and how to draft strong, appropriate information privacy policies and procedures are useful skills for librarians, for other information professionals, and for those seeking such positions in today's competitive job market. The importance of information privacy policies, considerations for drafting policies, and building a strong privacy program are considered in this chapter.

Over-collection of personal information can be a problem especially where safeguards on retained information may be lax and put this information at further risk. Storing personal data that is not needed for the functioning of a company or other entity also does not make good business sense. Therefore, information collection, integrity, retention, security, and workflow should be examined. Determining who has and who needs to have access to private information should be carefully scrutinized. The fewer employees and third parties accessing personal data, the safer it will be.

Before creating or updating a privacy policy or policies, it is important to examine the entity's information privacy practices. Map where and how data is being used. It must be determined whether personal information collection is necessary as well as where and how data is collected, used, and stored. How long is personal information being retained and for what purpose? Who is doing the collecting? What security measures are in place? Are the security measures reasonable in light of the sensitivity of the information and the risk of data breach? How long is information kept and how and when is it destroyed? Is personal information being used by or shared with third parties such as vendors or contractors? Contracts should be carefully examined to determine if they permit information sharing outside of the company and what protections are in place for that information. Has data collection, use, storage, and protection been examined for all business units or sections? All sections of a business must be examined. While information technology and security departments may be able to identify the bulk of the systems that use, collect, and store personal data, there may be other areas.

PRIVACY POLICIES

Every entity that collects information should provide its privacy policy to customers and users. Not only does this policy serve as a statement of your entity's data practices, but it also assures the user or customer that the entity takes privacy seriously. Providing a well-written privacy policy that explains what information is being collected, how the information is used, and with whom it may be shared can instill a feeling of confidence that it is safe to share personal information. The importance of such a policy has been highlighted by the recent reported data breaches at Target[1] and Neiman Marcus[2] and the revelations of large-scale surveillance by the NSA. People want to know what personal information companies are collecting, what they are doing with this information, and what they are doing to secure it.

A feeling of safety is especially important in libraries, where many individuals go to access the Internet, as well as in healthcare organizations, where patients expect protection of the personal information they share with their doctors, and federal law specifically prohibits its disclosure in certain circumstances.[3] Having and following a privacy policy makes for good customer relations for all organizations and sends a message to any regulating agency that privacy is a priority and that laws relating to privacy are being obeyed.[4]

Businesses often have multiple privacy policies for a variety of reasons including different data collection techniques, separate policies for websites, physical locations, or differing services, and separate policies for employees and customers. There may be specific privacy policies that address functions for specific areas in an organization. For example, there may be privacy policies related to the handling of health information in human resources departments and technology-related privacy and security policies residing in IT departments.[5]

Some privacy policies are internal only and serve to guide those working in a company while others are designed to inform both internal and external audiences.[6] Even policies directed to and shared with customers and other outside individuals must be understood and supported by employees. It is also crucial that external facing policies and internal procedures align. Anything that is stated in the privacy policy that customers or users rely on must be practiced internally. While privacy policies and programs are addressed separately below, it should be noted that in practice the two are connected. Privacy policies are generally thought of as the external facing policies provided to customers and users. Privacy programs encompass all of an entity's privacy practices including both external and internal policies, procedures, and actions necessary to ensure privacy. Internal actions include the alignment of business procedures, the creation of privacy checklists, creation of internal privacy policies, assessments, training, compliance monitoring, and more.

Start with the Law

One of the first steps in preparing to write a privacy policy is to investigate and understand the laws that apply to the company or information environment. What limits or requirements are placed on the collection, use, and handling of information in that environment? As mentioned in chapter 3, there are laws that apply to certain sectors including health, education, financial, government, and commercial websites that collect information from children under age 13. Other actions are also regulated, such as telemarketing and telecommunications.

Laws that impact privacy and are applicable but not specific to a business sector should also be considered such as FISA and the USA PATRIOT Act. Although the actual release of a person's private information under these Acts may not be reported to the individual, users should be warned in advance that information could be released in accordance with these laws. Any events that would lead to the release of personal data must be considered and addressed in the policy, including the release of information in response to a subpoena or under applicable state or federal laws.

Track and Evaluate Data Collection, Use, and Risk

Tracking and evaluating how your organization collects, uses, stores, shares, secures, and disposes of data is a necessary initial step in planning a privacy policy. Employees from all divisions must be consulted and enlisted to help determine where data is housed and how it is used. In certain organizations information may be collected and/or housed outside of the company. Examining contracts to determine which vendors or contractors, if any, are collecting or housing information on behalf of the organization and determining that the contractual privacy and confidentiality clauses meet legal and organizational standards is an important initial step.

Perform a Privacy Audit or Assessment

Performing a privacy audit, or assessment of how an organization manages privacy risks, is often the best means to get a baseline assessment of how well the organization is protecting data and following its privacy policies and procedures. Performing a privacy audit involves assessing all documentation addressing information privacy protection. This includes the evaluation of all privacy policies, procedures, and checklists, as well as provisions in contracts with third parties who may have access to PII. How data flows through an organization is mapped and data handling practices are assessed to determine if they comply with legal requirements and industry best practices. Audits may also focus on compliance, determining how well an organization is following its own policies and procedures. Privacy audits can determine areas for improvement and identify gaps in protection or compliance.[7]

Audits can also assist with risk management by helping organizations identify, assess, and prioritize risks to data. Keith P. Enright, Chief Privacy Officer for Lucira Technologies Inc., offers a checklist and questions to consider during the process to assist auditors.[8] Other templates for audits and assessments are available online and can serve as a starting point. Even if privacy policies and protections are already in place, a privacy audit is a smart choice. Periodic audits can help assess the health of a privacy program and determine whether staff or employees are complying with privacy policies.

Explain What You Collect and How You Use Personal Data

Users, customers, browsers, and anyone else who may have their information collected or used will want to know who is collecting it, why they are collecting it, and how it is being collected and used. They want to have a choice about sharing information and to be able to make an informed decision about whether to share their information. People also want to know that their data is protected. While it may be true that many people do not read privacy policies in their entirety, this speaks more to the dense and lengthy formats typical of such policies than it does to users' desires to be informed about how their data is collected and used. Businesses should keep in mind fair information practice principles[9] as determinations are made about what data to collect and how it will be used and shared. Thought should be given as to how to present privacy policies in accessible, user-friendly ways.

Collecting and Sharing Information: Cookie Use and Third Parties

If cookies are used to track users, this should be clearly explained in language that is easy to understand. If sharing of information is needed to complete certain processes, this too must be clearly explained. Users have the right to know and make an informed decision about whether to share their information with third parties. Use plain language to explain collection, tracking, and sharing, and include clear headings in the privacy policy to identify where the information can be found. It should not take twenty minutes of searching to locate the sections of a privacy policy that address these issues.

Contact Information

One of the failings of several online websites is not providing easy-to-locate contact information. Few things are more frustrating to a website visitor than finding that his or her information has been shared online and then wasting time searching for the means to contact someone to file a complaint or request that their information be removed. In an age where a user's personal information can be made too freely accessible, the means to contact the person or department in order to opt-out of sharing or to have information removed should not be difficult to locate.

Plain Language

The move to use plain language in an easy-to-read format is one that has been touted in the federal government for several years.[10] This message is also imparted by FTC staff and simply makes good sense. Users want to be able to read and easily understand how their information is being collected, used, and disclosed. No one should have to go to law school to understand a privacy policy. Jargon should be removed from the policy statements to make it accessible to everyone. Privacy policies should always be written at reading and comprehension levels that are comfortable for their target audiences. Kinsella Media advises drafters of privacy policies to present the material in a "question and answer format" to make the material most understandable.[11]

Visual Cues

Visual cues can also help readers to quickly hone in on the areas of most interest to them. In March of 2014 Lookout, a San Francisco-based mobile security company, launched *Private Parts*, "an open-sourced, customizable toolkit" for creating privacy policies that are "user-friendly" and include visual cues to help users identify the subject of the section. Lookout's toolkit stems from their implementation of the National Telecommunications and Information Agency (NTIA)'s code of conduct for mobile application transparency. It is focused on transparency and clarity.[12] The inclusion of visual cues does not need to be limited to application privacy policies. It could be implemented for other types of privacy policies and serve as a way to ease language barriers.

Layered Policies (Also Known as Layered Notices)

Layered policy explanations can help demystify privacy policies for users while still providing notice to them of policy terms. A good layered policy allows a reader to understand the basics of the privacy policy in a top-layer summary with links to access the full privacy policy. Some of the best layered policies have links that guide readers to more discussion of specific sections without having to sift through a lengthy policy in search of the relevant material. Some offer FAQ sections to provide quick answers to common privacy-related questions. The Center for Information Policy Leadership recommends having multilayered policies because these policies help develop trust among consumers and regulators. They also note that short notices, the initial condensed policy, can be translated into multiple languages.[13] This can be especially useful for entities with customers or users who speak different languages.

Prominently Display Your Privacy Policy and Opt-Out Choice

Privacy policies should be prominently displayed where users and customers expect to see them. Placing a link to the policy in a highly visible area on the home page is a good idea. Providing links to the privacy policy from several different locations is helpful. Including a link to the privacy policy from all pages is a way to ensure that users can access it at all times. A user may also seek answers contained in the privacy policy under a help link or an FAQs section. It is recommended that in addition to posting your opt-out options in email marketing, these options be displayed in your policy and readily accessible to users of your website.[14]

Contract for the Same Level of Privacy

Statements made in an organization's privacy policies are generally binding regardless of where the information is housed. This is a strong motivation for your organization to ensure that everyone with access to personal data obeys the provisions of the organization's privacy policies. This includes vendors, contractors, and anyone else who may have access to personal information collected. Therefore, when contracting with third parties that collect personal data of users or patrons, your organization must make sure that proper privacy protections are in place. These include data protection and confidentiality clauses in the contracting agreement. Protections must conform to the terms in the privacy policy.

Potential vendors or contractors should be investigated to determine if they have any history of privacy or security violations, if they adhere to contract terms, and for their general reputations. Entities may wish to include contract provisions that allow for inspections or audits to determine if adequate protections are in place to safeguard information and if contract terms are being fulfilled. Contract terms must clearly provide for privacy and security of personal data at or greater than the level specified in the privacy policy or policies.

Review Good Examples of Privacy Policies

One of the easiest ways to make your own privacy policies user-friendly is to view examples of good policies and use them as guides to create policies that work for your institution. Several good examples have been highlighted by members of the International Association of Privacy Professionals. These include McAfee's privacy policy,[15] which includes a layered notice, an audio version of the privacy notice, a link to download the policy, and a "tour" that includes visual cues, making it easier for visual learners and nonnative speakers. The privacy policy from Publishers Clearinghouse[16] is a good example of a policy that presents the information in a user-friendly manner that will be accessible to users of differing educational levels. It includes short-format notices, icons, and hypertext links to learn more in each section. Those seeking examples of simpler policies may be interested in reviewing the privacy policy of Sense Networks,[17] which includes two columns, one that presents the policy and a corresponding column titled "What This Means" that presents the concept in a shorter format, making it easy to read and skim. Many other good examples are available on the Internet.

Get Key Employees and Executives Involved

In preparation for drafting privacy policies and implementing a privacy program, employees from different divisions must be consulted and enlisted to help determine where data is housed and how it is used. Strong privacy programs have the support of upper management and executives. These individuals shape opinions, control the funding, and can make a program successful through their endorsement of and commitment to it. It is important to get such leaders involved.[18] Their visible support is crucial to creating a business culture that respects privacy, devotes adequate resources to a privacy program, and recognizes the importance of creating policies that adhere to law, regulation, and recommended privacy practices.

Review, Approval, and Implementation

Once a privacy policy has been drafted, the next step is to submit it for review by legal counsel. It is helpful to include the laws, policies, procedures, and any other materials relied on in the formation of the policy. Librarians may want to include reference to their ethical codes as part of the background materials for the creation and approval of library privacy policies. If the privacy policy is being drafted without the help of a privacy professional, a privacy consultation may be warranted. Privacy consultants can work with your organization's staff throughout the process to perform privacy assessments, draft policies, develop information risk management strategies, and advise on privacy and information management generally. They can support, manage, and help execute privacy programs.

PRIVACY PROGRAMS

Having a privacy policy is just a beginning step. In order to carry out the goal of ensuring the information privacy of customers or users, a privacy program is needed to operationalize the statements contained in the policy. Just as with creating the policies, when creating a privacy program, starting with the law is a smart choice. The legal and regulatory requirements will help define the scope of the program.

Managing information privacy is a matter of managing risk. No program can perfectly protect privacy *and* allow free access and use. Efforts must be made to maximize security and privacy of personal data while still supporting the mission and goals of the entity. It is important to know not only which laws apply in your work environment but also the penalties for non-compliance. Management should always be informed of the possible penalties while developing the overarching strategy to protect information privacy.

Support and Strategic Planning

Education and persuasion are the tools for gaining support. Stakeholders are some of the first individuals for whom a privacy workshop should be conducted. Once they are on board, privacy education can be more broadly embraced. Not everyone is as informed on information privacy issues and particularly those who do not work in the information professions, law, security, or privacy may benefit from additional instruction to help form a foundation on which continuing information privacy education can be built. Highlighting key privacy initiatives and their importance while providing foundational instruction is necessary to increase awareness.

Once a privacy program is up and running, steps must be taken to keep it going and to ensure the health of the program. Creating a strategic vision for the privacy program and getting others involved and invested in it is key to keeping the momentum going. Tying privacy to the basic goals and vision of the entity will help promote privacy goals and help integrate them into the organization's culture.

Training and Awareness

Privacy training should be incorporated into the work life of employees from the hiring stage forward. This applies to full-time employees, contractors, and volunteers. Everyone working for the institution should have a copy of the privacy policy and understand the organization's privacy practices. It is important to remember that people have different learning styles and that implementing different types of training can be helpful in employee comprehension of privacy policies and procedures. Some people benefit from in-person training; others prefer to read the material on their own. Many individuals enjoy interactive learning; still others may be primarily auditory learners. Providing multiple methods to learn about information privacy policies and procedures can help employees assimilate the information. Ongoing privacy training should remain a priority as every member of staff will need to understand current privacy practices and how to implement them on the job.

Distribution of procedures and checklists also should help implement the policy. A downfall of many policies is the lack of established practical procedures, checklists, and ongoing training to make sure that employees understand and remember over time how to carry out the provisions of the privacy policy. It can only be effective if it is implemented. Employees should be accountable for implementing the privacy practices of the institution. Periodic specialized training sessions focused on the work of individual business units and building in accountability measures in performance plans can help ensure that privacy is a high priority.

Employees must be made aware of the possible disciplinary actions that can arise from failing to abide by privacy and security policies and procedures. This may include a verbal or written warning with follow-up education or even suspension or termination if the severity of the action warrants it and the disciplinary action is deemed appropriate by management, human resources, and legal counsel.

Privacy Policies, Procedures, Checklists

Making sure that privacy practices within the organization are aligned with what is stated in the publicized privacy policy is imperative. Written policies, procedures, and checklists provide guidance to employees and others about how personal data is protected. Clearly, they must be consistent and comply with applicable law and regulation. This requires careful documentation and clear and consistent writing to ensure that procedures make sense to employees and can be carried out.

An October 2013 news article reported that a hospital laptop containing patient medical records in Vermont was given to a former employee to fix.[19] While it is not known how the laptop containing sensitive information was allowed to leave the premises, it highlights the importance of having privacy and security programs in place with clear policies, procedures, checklists, and periodic audits to track data flows and dictate data sharing, retention, and destruction practices. Many large agencies and companies use checklists as part of their documentation for equipment in the possession of employees and to assure the return of those items when employees leave the company.

It is not uncommon to have and keep lists of access rights and company equipment held by each employee and to revoke access rights and have all equipment returned at the end of service. The return of equipment is witnessed and checked off to be certain that security is not compromised. The Vermont incident calls into question whether such security measures were in place at the hospital.

Creating a Privacy Team

Selecting staff to join a privacy team should be done carefully, leveraging the skills of team members and selecting individuals who will promote a vision of privacy that conforms to law and regulation, the institution's privacy policies, and privacy best practices. Depending on the size of the institution, it may be prudent to select team members who can implement privacy measures in their departments or units. The privacy work done by these individuals must be integrated into their performance plans, job descriptions, or both. Value must be placed on this duty and opportunities for advancement with a privacy focus in the institution must be made available to keep strong performers and ensure program continuity.

Challenges

Data must be tracked across the organization and through the data lifecycle. A privacy framework must be built that includes the establishment of responsibility for securing and properly handling data. Data inventories are needed. They must be maintained and updated regularly. Knowing where personal data resides (on laptops, desktops, tablets, and servers in files, databases, and applications) is crucial to ensuring the security, management, and assessment of risk of this information. It is also necessary for accountability. Individuals and departments responsible for safeguarding information must be identified and a system must be established to detect unauthorized access or breaches of established privacy and security policies and procedures.

Monitoring regulations and privacy resources is part of managing a privacy program. When laws change and new laws are created that impact how a company can use data, this information must be known, and policies and practices must change to reflect it. The same is true of security and technological advances that may be integrated into the privacy and security framework. The program as a whole will need to maintain flexibility to accommodate new laws, regulations, technological advances, and guidance.

Privacy team members may also be called on to develop means to measure performance and will need to document any changes to the policy, training, and any new initiatives. Documentation must be kept in a state of readiness for possible audit or investigation. The role of the privacy professional and that of the privacy team member require critical thinking, an attention to detail, organization, and the ability to bridge professional differences to motivate individuals working in different divisions and disciplines to work together to ensure the privacy and security of personal data.

Communication

It is important not only to provide training but also to remain open and available to communicate with employees. Regular interaction with employees is needed to keep information privacy a priority. The chief privacy person or privacy point of contact should be available to discuss privacy matters and provide advice when needed. If employees do not feel comfortable speaking with a privacy officer, they are less likely to engage until they encounter problems. Remaining open and furthering discussions can allow small problems to be addressed before they grow into larger ones. It can also cultivate a community of employees interested in furthering privacy practices at the institution.

Incident Reporting and Response

It is important to set up a process for reporting and documenting incidents and contacting the privacy officer or office when problems are detected. Appointing a privacy point of contact for business units in a large organization can help in prompt reporting and response. Procedures should be established and readily accessible to assist employees in reporting, documenting, and responding to privacy incidents. Those working in organizations that maintain an intranet should consider including a designated privacy office site with contact information, policies, procedures, privacy frequently asked questions, and information about how to recognize and report incidents. The International Association of Privacy Professionals defines a data breach as "the unauthorized acquisition of computerized data that compromises the security, confidentiality, or integrity of personal information maintained by a data collector."[20] Unauthorized access of computerized data that compromises or has likely compromised the security, confidentiality, or integrity of personal information may also be considered a breach. Breaches may be intentional or accidental. Incidents may not rise to the level of being breaches but they must be promptly reported and responded to so that a determination can be made if a breach has occurred.

Data Breach

Have a plan in place in the event of a data breach. Determine how breaches will be handled and who will be in charge of what functions. Assign alternates to the front line personnel and, where feasible, secondary alternates. Keep everyone, including top management, aware of data breach response plans. Have practice sessions on how to handle a data breach. Jay Cline, the principal of Data Protection and Privacy at Price Waterhouse Coopers, and Chris Zoladz, the founder of Navigate LLC, recommend staging tabletop sessions that simulate hypothetical but realistic breach scenarios with personnel who will be responsible for responding to the breach. The goal of these sessions is to determine weaknesses in your policies, procedures, checklists, and overall breach plan.[21]

Plans will vary depending on the size of the company and the number of individuals impacted. Some things to consider before a breach occurs are: Who in the company must be notified once a breach is detected and what will they do? Who will be in charge if primary personnel are unavailable? How will the company notify those impacted by the breach? Is the contact information for these individuals current?

Determining ahead of time what mechanisms will be used to provide customers with additional answers to their questions such as an FAQs page and a phone number to call can help instill confidence.[22] Consideration should be given to what forms of compensation may be offered to an injured party. Will credit monitoring be provided? If so, examining options before a breach and having a plan to provide the service quickly is in order. Companies may want to consider data breach insurance. A recent breach at the University of Maryland[23] is expected to cost the institution millions of dollars. Breach insurance can help offset these costs and insurers offer insurance and services to help companies meet regulatory requirements and handle data breaches.[24]

LIBRARY PRIVACY POLICIES AND PROGRAMS

Libraries must consider the unique and varied needs of their patrons, many of whom may not be privacy literate, and are therefore more likely to engage in conduct that results in a loss of information privacy. Public libraries play a pivotal role in providing access to information for children, immigrants and nonnative speakers, and those without Internet access in their homes. School libraries also meet the information needs of children. These library users may need training in privacy and extra assistance in understanding privacy issues and policies.

All libraries should have privacy policies in place to let users know their data collection, use, security, and sharing practices. It bears repeating that privacy policies should explain in plain language what information is being collected, why, how the information is used, how it is secured, and with whom it may be shared by the library. The conditions under which information may be shared should be clearly outlined. Information addressing the purging of records should also be included. Providing this information in a privacy policy that is visible and easy to read can instill a feeling of confidence that it is safe to share information. Privacy policies should also inform patrons of the risk of using library computers to share personal information.

Language and Presentation Options

Libraries serving users and communities where English is not the primary language should consider offering privacy policies in more than one language. Users whose first language is not English may have more difficulty understanding how their information will be collected and used if the notice is not also provided in their native language. The principles mentioned above of using plain language including visual cues and layering notices can help to simplify policies.

Privacy policies should be prominently displayed in libraries. Users of all libraries should have easy options to view the privacy policy. Policies should be available on the library's websites. One option that can be used for computer users is to post the privacy policy on an intial screen or include the link prominently on initial or log-in screens for computers. Library staff should also use opportunities such as initial registration for library cards, library card renewals, computer sign-ups, and the scheduling of meeting-room reservations to share copies of the library's privacy policy with patrons. Privacy Awareness Week[25] is also a great time to talk with patrons about privacy, the library's privacy policy, and why safeguarding personal information is important.

Considerations before Drafting

Data Flows and Retention

Just as with other types of entities, it is important for libraries to carefully consider what information they are collecting from patrons and the necessity of this collection. Current practices should be reviewed to determine if the amount of information being collected can be reduced. Policies and procedures governing the length of record retention should also be examined. Record retention practices concerning individual patron records, records generated containing patron information, and search logs should be examined. Libraries should strive to provide the maximum protection legally possible to patrons' personal information and this includes eliminating records of patron information including patron actions where feasible. Records should be retained only for as long as needed to perform library functions or as required by law.

Data Collection, Use, and Third Parties

The goal should be to collect the least amount of information possible to perform library functions and provide services. Forms used to collect information should be examined to determine if information collection can be reduced. These include but are not limited to library card applications, patron holds, Internet use sign-up sheets, sign-up sheets for other library services, and interlibrary loan requests. Policies and procedures addressing operational functions should be written with a focus on patron privacy examining both the information privacy and physical privacy of patrons.

Careful examination of the technologies used in the library should be made to determine what information is being collected, how it is being used, and how it is being stored. Third-party access to personal information of patrons should be examined and minimized. Vendor portals or other third-party services may collect PII from patrons. It is the library's duty to make sure that adequate privacy protections are in place and are part of the contract terms with vendors. It is also recommended that vendors be investigated to determine if they have any history of privacy or security violations. Inspections or audits may also be considered. Academic and public libraries especially will want to pay careful attention to the terms of the library's contracts with third-party service providers such as electronic publishers and database providers whose services may be accessed by patrons outside of the library. Terms of the contracts must clearly provide for privacy and security of patron personal information at a level that meets the requirements of the library's privacy policy.

Awareness and Training

Staff should keep abreast of the latest security and privacy protections as well as changes in technology. Security and privacy issues must be considered when integrating new technology into libraries such as RFID devices. Designated staff should continue reading and learning about technology, privacy, and security to remain current. Privacy and security training should be provided regularly for all staff, students, volunteers, and anyone else working in a paid or unpaid capacity in the library. Continuing training on applicable laws and how to handle privacy incidents is needed as well.

Considerations for Special Populations

In addition to the general privacy considerations for a library environment as discussed in this chapter and chapter 5, a major consideration for public libraries is the training of patrons about how to keep their personal data private and secure. Libraries provide services to several populations that may need additional training and awareness efforts concerning information privacy. These include children, immigrants and nonnative speakers, and the elderly. These groups along with the many patrons who rely on the library as their primary source for online access may not be as aware of the dangers of releasing personal information and may more easily be persuaded to act in ways that are detrimental to their privacy. Special efforts should be made to provide them with training and to discuss the library's privacy policy and how it affects the collection and handling of their private information. More information about the content of privacy training can be found in chapter 4.

ALA Guidance for Libraries

The ALA's Office of Intellectual Freedom has created a body of useful information to guide libraries in the creation of library privacy policies. This information, found in the *Privacy Toolkit*,[26] is available on their website. The toolkit provides guidance for developing a library privacy policy and includes a link to the ALA's model library privacy policy.

CONCLUSION

Developing sound information privacy policies requires an understanding of the laws, regulations, and best practices. It requires an assessment of privacy risks. Privacy policies must comply with law and institutional practices and must be understandable to readers. Anyone creating or updating privacy policies should examine the existing data collection practices of their environment. It is important to understand what personal data is being collected and how it is being used, shared, stored, protected, and destroyed.

Privacy training and awareness is important for everyone. It should be personalized when possible and provided in a variety of formats to assist those with different learning styles. Everyone working in or using a particular environment should have a copy of the privacy policy and understand the institution's privacy practices. Privacy programs help institutions keep abreast of privacy changes, comply with laws, protect data privacy, create accountability in organizations, document privacy efforts, and support privacy best practices. The creation of a privacy program requires strong institutional support.

Every library should have a public privacy policy to let users know their data collection, use, sharing, and security practices. Privacy training and awareness is important for everyone working in the library and for the library's patrons to understand how to keep personal information secure. The ALA offers information to guide libraries in the creation of library privacy policies and best practices.

Anyone embarking on an information privacy project, whether to create a privacy policy or to implement a privacy program, can benefit from consulting with a privacy expert. Hiring someone who understands the laws, the issues, and how to implement privacy programs can save time and establish a firm foundation on which to grow. Privacy consultants can help guide businesses and libraries as they create user-friendly privacy policies and privacy programs.

NOTES

1. Elizabeth Harris and Nicole Perloth, " Target Missed Signs of a Data Breach," *New York Times*, March 13, 2014, available online at www.nytimes.com/2014/03/14/business/target-missed-signs-of-a-data-breach.html?_r=0.

2. Ben Elgin, Dune Lawrence, and Michael Riley, "Neiman Marcus Hackers Set Off 60,000 Alerts While Bagging Credit Card Data," *Bloomberg BusinessWeek*, February 21, 2014, available online at www.businessweek.com/articles/2014-02-21/neiman-marcus-hackers-set-off-60-000-alerts-while-bagging-credit-card-data.

3. National Research Council, *Beyond the HIPAA Privacy Rule: Enhancing Privacy, Improving Health through Research* (Washington, DC: The National Academies Press, 2009), 77.

4. White House, *Consumer Data Privacy in a Networked World: A Framework for Protecting Privacy and Promoting Innovation in the Global Digital Economy* (Washington, DC: The White House, 2012), 29.

5. Russell Densmore, ed., *Privacy Program Management: Tools for Managing Privacy within Your Organization* (Portsmouth, NH: International Association of Privacy Professionals, 2013), 13–14.

6. An example of a privacy policy that provides information to both internal and external audiences is Agrium's employee privacy policy, available at www.agrium.com/employee_privacy.jsp. Agrium's policy addresses the privacy of current employees, past employees, and those seeking employment with Algium.

7. Michael Whitener, "Conducting a Privacy Audit," *Corporate Counselor* 27, no. 3 (July 2012), available online at www.lawjournalnewsletters.com/issues/ljn_corpcounselor/26_7/pdf/156861-1.html.

8. Keith P. Enright, "Privacy Audit Checklist," Berkman Center for Internet and Society at Harvard University, March 16, 2014, http://cyber.law.harvard.edu/ecommerce/privacyaudit.html.

9. Eight principles currently form the foundation of fair information practice in the United States. They are: transparency, individual participation, purpose specification, data minimization, use limitation, data quality and integrity, security, and accountability and auditing. These principles are addressed in greater depth in chapter 7.

10. Federal agencies have been striving to provide clear communication that the public can understand and use in accordance with the Plain Writing Act of 2010.

11. Kinsella Media, "Plain Language Primer for Privacy Policies," accessed March 16, 2014, www.kinsellamedia.com/LinkClick.aspx?fileticket=aYdiFrXak_4%3D&tabid=200.

12. Lookout conducted a survey of two thousand users to determine how they feel about privacy policies and created a new format. Ric Velez, "Lookout Open Sourced Its 'Private Parts,' You Should, Too," *Lookout*, March 12, 2014, https://blog.lookout.com/blog/2014/03/12/open-source-privacy-policy.

13. The Center for Information Policy Leadership, "Ten Steps to Develop a Multilayered Privacy Notice," Hunton and Williams LLP, March 19, 2014, www.informationpolicycentre.com/files/Uploads/Documents/Centre/Ten_Steps_whitepaper.pdf, 3.

14. Caron Beesley, "7 Considerations for Crafting an Online Privacy Policy," U.S. Small Business Administration, June 26, 2012, www.sba.gov/community/blogs/community-blogs/business-law-advisor/7-considerations-crafting-online-privacy-policy.

15. "McAfee Privacy Notice," McAfee, March 19, 2014, www.mcafee.com/common/privacy/english/index.htm.

16. "Publishers Clearinghouse Privacy Policy," Publishers Clearinghouse, http://privacy.pch.com (accessed March 14, 2014).

17. "Privacy Policy," Sense Networks, March 19, 2014, www.sensenetworks.com/principles/privacy-policy.

18. Densmore, *Privacy Program Management*, 11–12.

19. Gina Bullard, "Dispute over Hospital Laptop Puts Patient Privacy at Risk," WCAX.com, October 14, 2013, www.wcax.com/story/23671159/dispute-over-hospital-laptop-puts-patient-privacy-at-risk.

20. International Association of Privacy Professionals, "Glossary," IAPP, March 19, 2014, www.privacyassociation.org/media/pdf/resource_center/IAPP%20Privacy%20Certification%20Glossary%202.1.0.2.pdf.

21. Jay Cline and Chris Zoladz, "Getting Results: 13 Proven Tips for Managing an Effective Privacy Program," presentation, Global Privacy Summit, Washington, DC, March 5, 2014.

22. Experian Data Breach Resolution, "Data Breach Case Study of Lesson from the Field," 2012, www.privacyassociation.org/media/pdf/knowledge_center/Data_Breach_Lessons_Learned__From_the_Field.pdf (accessed March 16, 2014).

23. Mike Denison, "University of Maryland's Response to Data Breach May Cost Millions," Capital News Service, February 28, 2014, http://cnsmaryland.org/2014/02/28/university-of-marylands-response-to-database-breach-may-cost-millions.

24. A number of companies offer data-breach insurance including the Hartford (www.thehartford.com/data-breach-insurance), TechInsurance (www.techinsurance.com/cyber-liability-insurance/data-breach-insurance), and HSB (www.hsb.com/HSBGroup/Data_Compromise.aspx).

25. Privacy Awareness Week is celebrated in countries across the globe including Australia, Canada, Hone Kong, Korea, Macau, Mexico, New Zealand, and the United States. For more information on Privacy Awareness Week, an initiative of the Asia Pacific Privacy Authorities forum (APPA), see www.privacyawarenessweek.org.

26. Office for Intellectual Freedom, "Privacy Toolkit," American Library Association, www.ala.org/offices/oif/iftoolkits/toolkitsprivacy/default (accessed March 16, 2014).

BIBLIOGRAPHY

Beesley, Caron. "7 Considerations for Crafting an Online Privacy Policy." U.S. Small Business Administration, June 26, 2012. www.sba.gov/community/blogs/community-blogs/business-law-advisor/7-considerations-crafting-online-privacy-policy.

Centre for Information Policy Leadership. "Ten Steps to Develop a Multilayered Privacy Notice." Hunton and Williams LLP, March 19, 2014. www.informationpolicycentre.com/files/Uploads/Documents/Centre/Ten_Steps_whitepaper.pdf.

Densmore, Russell, ed. *Privacy Program Management: Tools for Managing Privacy within Your Organization.* Portsmouth, NH: International Association of Privacy Professionals, 2013.

Elgin, Ben, Dune Lawrence, and Michael Riley. "Neiman Marcus Hackers Set Off 60,000 Alerts While Bagging Credit Card Data." Bloomberg BusinessWeek, February 21, 2014. Available online at www.businessweek.com/articles/2014-02-21/neiman-marcus-hackers-set-off-60-000-alerts-while-bagging-credit-card-data.

Experian Data Breach Resolution. "Data Breach Case Study of Lesson from the Field." 2012. www.privacyassociation.org/media/pdf/knowledge_center/Data_Breach_Lessons_Learned__From_the_Field.pdf (accessed March 16, 2014).

Harris, Elizabeth, and Nicole Perloth. "Target Missed Signs of a Data Breach." *New York Times*, March 13, 2014. Available online at www.nytimes.com/2014/03/14/business/target-missed-signs-of-a-data-breach.html?_r=0.

Herath, Kirk, ed. *Building a Privacy Policy: A Practitioner's Guide.* Portsmouth, NH: International Association of Privacy Professionals, 2011.

Kinsella Media, LLC. "Plain Language Primer for Privacy Policies." Kinsella Media LLC, n.d. www.kinsellamedia.com/LinkClick.aspx?fileticket=aYdiFrXak_4%3D&tabid=200.

National Research Council. *Beyond the HIPAA Privacy Rule: Enhancing Privacy, Improving Health through Research* . Washington, DC: The National Academies Press, 2009.

Office for Intellectual Freedom. "Privacy Toolkit." American Library Association, March 16, 2014. www.ala.org/offices/oif/iftoolkits/toolkitsprivacy/default.

Plain Writing Act of 2010, H. R. 946/Public Law 111–274.

White House. *Consumer Data Privacy in a Networked World: A Framework for Protecting Privacy and Promoting Innovation in the Global Digital Economy.* Washington, DC: The White House, 2012.

Whitener, Michael. "Conducting a Privacy Audit." *Corporate Counselor* 27, no. 3 (July 2012). Available online at www.lawjournalnewsletters.com/issues/ljn_corpcounselor/26_7/pdf/156861-1.html.

Chapter Seven

Global Information Privacy

It is not enough to know the fundamentals of information privacy in the United States. We live and work in an age of global access to information. Personal data is being transferred across borders from one country to another. Companies have offices across the globe, and understanding how to fairly handle personal data and the duties owed to those whose information is being processed is a necessity. Everyone working with personal data needs to understand and apply fair information privacy practices.

Several international associations have sought to establish information privacy norms within certain areas of the world. These include the Organisation for Economic Co-operation and Development (OECD), the Council of Europe, the European Union (EU), and the Asia-Pacific Economic Cooperation (APEC). The United States and many other countries have created or adopted fair information principles. Depending on your work environment, it will be important to familiarize yourself with one or more of these organizations and their guidance concerning privacy. Anyone transferring or receiving data from other countries on a regular basis should learn about the privacy laws applicable in those countries. Understanding and being able to apply recognized fair information privacy practices is necessary for responsible handling of personal information and is needed to meet certain adequacy requirements to allow for the transfer of personal data across borders.

FAIR INFORMATION PRINCIPLES

The concept of fair information principles (FIPs) took root in the United States in the 1970s in response to the growing use of computers and the collection and use of personal data. The generally recognized principles of today stem from a 1973 report by the U.S. Department of Health, Education and Welfare's advisory committee on Automated Personal Data Systems.[1] The committee found that an individual's privacy was "poorly protected" under the law and existing record keeping practices. The committee recommended enactment of a federal code of information practice. It set forth five basic principles for the code. These are:

1. There must be no personal data record keeping systems whose very existence is secret.
2. There must be a way for an individual to find out what information about him is in a record and how it is used.
3. There must be a way for an individual to prevent information about him that was obtained for one purpose from being used or made available for other purposes without his consent.
4. There must be a way for an individual to correct or amend a record of identifiable information about him.
5. Any organization creating, maintaining, using, or disseminating records of identifiable personal data must assure the reliability of the data for their intended use and must take precautions to prevent misuse of the data.[2]

These FIPs are at the core of the Privacy Act of 1974,[3] which serves to regulate the collection, use, and disclosure of personal information contained in the U.S. government system of records. They provided the foundation for federal and state laws in the United States. They have also influenced the development of international guidelines such as the Organisation for Economic Co-operation and Development's *Guidelines Governing the Protection of Privacy and Transborder Data Flows of Personal Data* (OECD Guidelines). The OECD Guidelines were published in 1980 and were revised in 2013.

THE ORGANIZATION FOR ECONOMIC CO-OPERATION AND DEVELOPMENT'S GUIDELINES

It is not surprising that the FIPs had an influence on the OECD Guidelines. The United States joined the OECD as one of the initial members in 1961. Current OECD members include Australia, Austria, Belgium, Canada, Chile, the Czech Republic, Denmark, Estonia, Finland, France, Germany, Greece, Hungary, Iceland, Ireland, Israel, Italy, Japan, Republic of Korea, Luxembourg, Mexico, Netherlands, New Zealand, Norway, Poland, Portugal, the Slovak Republic, Slovenia, Spain, Sweden, Switzerland, Turkey, the United Kingdom, and the United States. The European Union also contributes to the work of the OECD.[4] The OECD Guidelines have been widely recognized and endorsed. According to Hugh G. Stephenson, the Deputy Director of the Office of International Affairs of the FTC, the OECD Guidelines have had an impact on federal laws in the United States.[5] Principles in the guidelines are also seen in the current Fair Information Practice Principles (FIPPs) of the United States, which are discussed below. These general principles that have their origins within the original FIPs form the widely recognized basis for fair information practices.

The eight basic principles of the 2013 OECD Guidelines© are:

1. *Collection Limitation Principle*: There should be limits to the collection of personal data and any such data should be obtained by lawful and fair means and, where appropriate, with the knowledge or consent of the data subject.
2. *Data Quality Principle*: Personal data should be relevant to the purposes for which they are to be used, and, to the extent necessary for those purposes, should be accurate, complete and kept up-to-date.
3. *Purpose Specification Principle*: The purposes for which personal data are collected should be specified not later than at the time of data collection and the subsequent use limited to the fulfilment of those purposes or such others as are not incompatible with those purposes and as are specified on each occasion of change of purpose.
4. *Use Limitation Principle*: Personal data should not be disclosed, made available or otherwise used for purposes other than those specified in accordance with . . . [the Purpose Specification Principle above] except:

    a. with the consent of the data subject;
    b. by the authority of law.

5. *Security Safeguards Principle*: Personal data should be protected by reasonable security safeguards against such risks as loss or unauthorised access, destruction, use, modification or disclosure of data.
6. *Openness Principle*: There should be a general policy of openness about developments, practices and policies with respect to personal data. Means should be readily available of establishing the existence and nature of personal data, and the main purposes of their use, as well as the identity and usual residence of the data controller.[6]
7. *Individual Participation Principle*: Individuals should have the right:

    a. to obtain from a data controller, or otherwise, confirmation of whether or not the data controller has data relating to them;

    b. to have communicated to them, data relating to them within a reasonable time; at a charge, if any, that is not excessive; in a reasonable manner; and in a form that is readily intelligible to them;

    c. to be given reasons if a request made under subparagraphs (a) and (b) is denied, and to be able to challenge such denial; and

    d. to challenge data relating to them and, if the challenge is successful to have the data erased, rectified, completed or amended.

8. *Accountability Principle*: A data controller should be accountable for complying with measures which give effect to the principles stated above.[7]

The OECD Guideline principles have helped to guide the establishment of other privacy frameworks and serve as basic levels of fair practice to be followed.

FAIR INFORMATION PRACTICE PRINCIPLES (USA)

In the United States the original FIPs were updated. Eight principles now form the foundation of fair information practice in the United States and expand on the original principles. They are: transparency, individual participation, purpose specification, data minimization, use limitation, data quality and integrity, security, and accountability and auditing. "FIPPs are the widely accepted framework of defining principles to be used in the evaluation and consideration of systems, processes, or programs that affect individual privacy."[8] In 2011, the White House included the updated version of the FIPs, known as the Fair Information Practice Principles (FIPPs) in its report, *National Strategy for Trusted Identities in Cyberspace: Enhancing Online Choice, Efficiency, Security, and Privacy.*[9] While these eight principles have been documented elsewhere, the White House statement is especially useful as it provides guidance on the meaning of each principle as it relates to organizations. Even the casual reader will note overlapping principles and language present in the OECD Guideline principles and the FIPPs. These general principles have been widely adapted by different countries and governing associations for their own use.

The FIPPs contained in the White House report are reproduced below:

1. *Transparency*: Organizations should be transparent and notify individuals regarding collection, use, dissemination, and maintenance of personally identifiable information (PII).

2. *Individual Participation*: Organizations should involve the individual in the process of using PII and, to the extent practicable, seek individual consent for the collection, use, dissemination, and maintenance of PII. Organizations should also provide mechanisms for appropriate access, correction, and redress regarding use of PII.

3. *Purpose Specification*: Organizations should specifically articulate the authority that permits the collection of PII and specifically articulate the purpose or purposes for which the PII is intended to be used.

4. *Data Minimization*: Organizations should only collect PII that is directly relevant and necessary to accomplish the specified purpose(s) and only retain PII for as long as is necessary to fulfill the specified purpose(s).

5. *Use Limitation*: Organizations should use PII solely for the purpose(s) specified in the notice. Sharing PII should be for a purpose compatible with the purpose for which the PII was collected.

6. *Data Quality >and Integrity*: Organizations should, to the extent practicable, ensure that PII is accurate, relevant, timely, and complete.

7. *Security*: Organizations should protect PII (in all media) through appropriate security safeguards against risks such as loss, unauthorized access or use, destruction, modification, or unintended or inappropriate disclosure.

8. *Accountability and Auditing*: Organizations should be accountable for complying with these principles, providing training to all employees and contractors who use PII, and auditing the actual use of PII to demonstrate compliance with these principles and all applicable privacy protection requirements. [10]

Both the principles in the OECD Guidelines and the White House statement of the FIPPs identify essentially the same eight principles and provide similar and in many cases overlapping guidance, though there are some differences that reflect the different privacy environments. Both sets of principles offer sound guidance for handing personal data.

EUROPEAN PRIVACY PROTECTIONS AND THE DATA PROTECTION DIRECTIVE

The OECD is not alone in offering guidance to European countries on the topic of personal data. The Council of Europe (COE) took visible steps in 1950 to ensure the privacy of Europeans. Echoing the Universal Declaration of Human Rights of 1948, mentioned in chapter 1, they reaffirmed the belief that individuals have fundamental freedoms in the Convention for the Protection of Human Rights and Fundamental Freedoms in 1950. Among those rights is the right to respect for privacy.[11] Building on this belief and with knowledge of the OECD Guidelines, the COE passed the Convention for the Protection of Individuals with Regard to Automatic Processing of Personal Data in 1981, which required that each party "take the necessary measures in its domestic law to give effect to the basic principles for data protection."[12]

Respect for private life and concern about fair practices to ensure protection of personal data have been further recognized in the EU Charter of Fundamental Rights, adopted in 2000 and reaffirmed in 2007. Articles 7 and 8 proclaim that both respect for private life and the protection of personal data are fundamental rights. The EU currently includes twenty-eight member countries: Austria, Belgium, Bulgaria, Croatia, Cyprus, Czech Republic, Denmark, Estonia, Finland, France, Germany, Greece, Hungary, Ireland, Italy, Latvia, Lithuania, Luxembourg, Malta, Netherlands, Poland, Portugal, Romania, Slovakia, Slovenia, Spain, Sweden, and the United Kingdom.[13]

These strong protections are reflected in the European Union Data Protection Directive. The directive, adopted in 1995, directs member states to adopt privacy laws that provide "equivalent protection" to remove impediments to the flow of personal data.[14] There have been recent efforts to reform the directive to provide those in the EU with more control over their own personal data and to make it easier for businesses in the EU to share personal data to conduct business. The European Parliament voted in favor of reform in a plenary vote on March 12, 2014. This means that support for the reform is solidified and anyone working with data from the EU should keep abreast of the changes that will be coming.[15] The move toward reform is not surprising. Concern about the safety of personal data of EU citizens remains high particularly in the wake of revelations about surveillance by the NSA. Members of EU countries have spoken about NSA surveillance and the need for assurances from the United States that EU data protection concerns will be addressed.[16]

U.S.-EU Safe Harbor Program

Currently, companies in the United States that meet certain criteria can participate in the U.S.-EU Safe Harbor program. The program allows them to self-certify that they meet the requirements to be deemed "adequate" under the EU Data Protection Directive in order to receive personal data from the 28 member states in the European Union. This registration to participate in the program is through the United States by the U.S. Department of Commerce. Organizations self-certify annually to participate. In order to be eligible, organizations must agree to abide by the U.S.-EU Safe Harbor Framework, which requires participating in a privacy program that adheres to the Safe Harbor Framework's requirements. The option is provided to join a self-regulatory privacy program or develop one. Organizations must comply with seven privacy principles. These are:

1. *Notice*: Organizations must notify individuals about the purposes for which they collect and use information about them. They must provide information about how individuals can contact the organization with any inquiries or complaints, the types of third parties to which it discloses the information and the choices and means the organization offers for limiting its use and disclosure.

2. *Choice*: Organizations must give individuals the opportunity to choose (opt out) whether their personal information will be disclosed to a third party or used for a purpose incompatible with the purpose for which it was originally collected or subsequently authorized by the individual. For sensitive information, affirmative or explicit (opt in) choice must be given if the information is to be disclosed to a third party or used for a purpose other than its original purpose or the purpose authorized subsequently by the individual.

3. *Onward Transfer (Transfers to Third Parties)*: To disclose information to a third party, organizations must apply the notice and choice principles. Where an organization wishes to transfer information to a third party that is acting as an agent, it may do so if it makes sure that the third party subscribes to the Safe Harbor Privacy Principles or is subject to the Directive or another adequacy finding. As an alternative, the organization can enter into a written agreement with such third party requiring that the third party provide at least the same level of privacy protection as is required by the relevant principles.

4. *Access*: Individuals must have access to personal information about them that an organization holds and be able to correct, amend, or delete that information where it is inaccurate, except where the burden or expense of providing access would be disproportionate to the risks to the individual's privacy in the case in question, or where the rights of persons other than the individual would be violated.

5. *Security*: Organizations must take reasonable precautions to protect personal information from loss, misuse and unauthorized access, disclosure, alteration and destruction.

6. *Data integrity*: Personal information must be relevant for the purposes for which it is to be used. An organization should take reasonable steps to ensure that data is reliable for its intended use, accurate, complete, and current.

7. *Enforcement*: In order to ensure compliance with the safe harbor principles, there must be (a) readily available and affordable independent

recourse mechanisms so that each individual's complaints and disputes can be investigated and resolved and damages awarded where the applicable law or private sector initiatives so provide; (b) procedures for verifying that the commitments companies make to adhere to the safe harbor principles have been implemented; and (c) obligations to remedy problems arising out of a failure to comply with the principles. Sanctions must be sufficiently rigorous to ensure compliance by the organization. Organizations that fail to provide annual self certification letters will no longer appear in the list of participants and Safe Harbor benefits will no longer be assured. [17]

Binding Corporate Rules and Model Contracts

Binding Corporate Rules (BCRs) are a means by which companies operating in more than one jurisdiction can demonstrate their commitment to adequate safeguards for the protection of the privacy of individuals. They are rules that are legally binding and must be approved by data protection authorities in the EU member countries in which the companies operate. BCRs were established as a means to comply with the EU Directive. [18]

Model contracts may be used as means to ensure the flow of personal data from a data controller in the EU or three other participating countries (Norway, Liechtenstein, Iceland) to a data controller or processer in an area not deemed to have its own adequate protections. The contractual clauses set the standard for handling personal data that meets the requirements of the Article 29 working group, [19] which was established under the EU Directive to protect the rights of individuals concerning the processing of their personal data. [20]

APEC PRIVACY FRAMEWORK

More recently, in 2004, the Asia-Pacific Economic Cooperation approved a privacy framework that sets out nine information privacy principles aligned with those of the OECD. The APEC is a multinational organization comprised of 21 members: Australia, Brunei Darussalam, Canada, Chile, China, Hong Kong, Indonesia, Japan, Republic of Korea, Malaysia, Mexico, New Zealand, New Guinea, Peru, the Philippines, Russia, Singapore, Chinese Taipei, Thailand, the United States, and Vietnam. [21] These countries have agreed to privacy principles in order to provide a flexible framework to govern the handling of private information. The approved principles were inspired by the OECD Guidelines and focus on preventing harm, limiting collection and use of personal information, providing notice, providing choice about collection where appropriate, maintaining the integrity of personal information and security safeguards, providing for access and correction, and ensuring for accountability when personal information is transferred. [22] APEC established the Cross-Border Privacy Rules (CBPR) system to implement their privacy framework. The CBPR system works to protect the privacy of personal data moving between APEC member countries by requiring companies transferring personal data to develop internal processes and rules to ensure privacy for the data transferred.[23]

CANADA'S MORE COMPREHENSIVE PROTECTIONS

While there is not sufficient space to address information efforts in every country in this short text, some portion must be dedicated to Canada as both Canadians and Americans are members of the American Library Association. ALA members from both countries share interests in privacy, literacy, professional ethics, and intellectual freedom. We can learn valuable insights examining the differences in their privacy approaches and the ways that Canadian privacy commissioners have sought to educate students and the public about information privacy.

Canada is an excellent example of a country that has embraced a more comprehensive approach to privacy compared with the United States, though Canada maintains a similar philosophy about working with businesses toward privacy compliance. Like the U.S. Constitution, *Canada's Charter of Rights and Freedoms* does not contain a specific reference to privacy, though sections 7 and 8 have been interpreted to offer privacy protections.

1. Everyone has the right to life, liberty and security of the person and the right not to be deprived thereof except in accordance with the principles of fundamental justice.
2. Everyone has the right to be secure against unreasonable search or seizure.[24]

Two Federal Laws

Canada has two main federal laws that govern the handling of personal data. They are the Privacy Act of 1983 and the Personal Information Protection and Electronic Documents Act of 2000 (PIPEDA). The Privacy Act applies to the handling of data by federal agencies and departments. It provides individuals with the right to access personal information about themselves in the possession of the government and to request correction when that information is incorrect. PIPEDA governs how organizations in the private sector can collect, use, and disclose personal data. Under PIPEDA individuals may also request access to the information collected about them and the correction of that information.[25]

PIPEDA Privacy Principles

PIPEDA was influenced by the OECD Guidelines and has 10 privacy principles, most of which mirror those discussed earlier in this chapter. They are:

1. *Accountability*: An organization is responsible for personal information under its control and shall designate an individual or individuals who are accountable for the organization's compliance with the following principles.
2. *Identifying Purposes*: The purposes for which personal information is collected shall be identified by the organization at or before the time the information is collected.
3. *Consent*: The knowledge and consent of the individual are required for the collection, use, or disclosure of personal information, except where inappropriate.
4. *Limiting Collection*: The collection of personal information shall be limited to that which is necessary for the purposes identified by the organization. Information shall be collected by fair and lawful means.
5. *Limiting Use, Disclosure, and Retention*: Personal information shall not be used or disclosed for purposes other than those for which it was collected, except with the consent of the individual or as required by law. Personal information shall be retained only as long as necessary for the fulfillment of those purposes.
6. *Accuracy*: Personal information shall be as accurate, complete, and up-to-date as is necessary for the purposes for which it is to be used.
7. *Safeguards*: Personal information shall be protected by security safeguards appropriate to the sensitivity of the information.
8. *Openness*: An organization shall make readily available to individuals specific information about its policies and practices relating to the management of personal information.
9. *Individual Access*: Upon request, an individual shall be informed of the existence, use, and disclosure of his or her personal information and shall be given access to that information. An individual shall be able to challenge the accuracy and completeness of the information and have it amended as appropriate.
10. *Challenging Compliance*: An individual shall be able to address a challenge concerning compliance with the above principles to the designated individual or individuals accountable for the organization's compliance.[26]

It is interesting to note the difference in language between the U.S. privacy principles and those of Canada. The U.S. language focuses on *should* whereas the Canadian principles use *shall*, much in the same way that the EU uses *must*. The Canadian principles are more forceful and comprehensive. The stronger language and protections are perhaps not too surprising when we consider that they are part of PIPEDA.[27] The strength of these protections warranted a finding by the EU in 2001 that certain personal data transferred from the EU to operators in Canada subject to PIPEDA was "adequately" protected.[28]

Canada's privacy commissioner is an officer of Parliament and fulfills the duty of protecting the privacy rights of Canadians through a number of measures including some that are similar to the functions of the FTC. The Commissioner investigates complaints, performs audits, and pursues legal remedies in the court. The Commissioner also serves as a source of information on practices for handling PII by both public- and private-sector organizations. Performing privacy research and increasing public awareness are also duties of the position.[29] She is assisted in some of these endeavors including public education by provincial information and privacy commissioners. The website of the Information and Privacy Commissioner of Ontario, Canada, provides a wealth of privacy information including extensive materials addressing "Privacy by Design."[30] Canadian public awareness efforts are exemplary and serve as guidance for those in the United States.

Canada's development of youthprivacy.ca and the creation and use of a graphic novel on privacy and Internet use,[31] student-centered privacy education videos, and presentation packages to teach youth about privacy establish that country as a leader in the arena of youth privacy literacy and should be a guide for other countries to follow. Launched in 2008 by the Office of the Privacy Commissioner of Canada (OPC), youthprivacy.ca is a wonderful resource that provides information directed to parents and teachers along with privacy activity sheets, videos for children, infographics, information about laws, and research, and presents information in both English and French. It should be a primary resource for anyone involved in privacy literacy in schools, public libraries, and even for those just seeking to learn more themselves or to teach friends and family members.

The OPC has several tools that are especially helpful for teaching adult privacy literacy including videos, podcasts, and information on topics such as identity theft, fraud, and how to file a complaint. The OPC website features privacy illustrations, a free privacy mobile application to help individuals protect their privacy on mobile devices, and general information about privacy including privacy laws. Information is available in English and French, with some Spanish content included as well. The OPC website also contains information for professionals including business owners seeking to create a privacy plan, information about compliance, and guidance concerning privacy breaches. The OPC is a leading source for information privacy education materials.[32]

CONCLUSION

FIPPs are well established. Understanding these principles and the variations among countries will help establish a good foundation for information handling. The documentation of the concept of fair information practices in the United States started in 1973 with a report by the U.S. Department of Health, Education and Welfare's advisory committee on Automated Personal Data Systems. The now generally recognized need to establish privacy principles for the handling of personal data followed on the heels of strides in the computer and data collection and processing.

The OECD Guidelines have been perhaps the most influential of the privacy frameworks and principles. These Guidelines have influenced federal and state laws in the United States and elsewhere, as well as other privacy frameworks, and share much in common in with privacy principles of the United States, the EU, the APEC, and Canada. Canadian privacy protections are more comprehensive than those in the United States. The efforts made by the Office of the Privacy Commissioner of Canada to educate youth and individuals of all ages about privacy can serve as an excellent model for those seeking to teach privacy literacy in the United States and elsewhere.

Practicing information privacy awareness, monitoring new developments, and implementing sound privacy practices are critical for all information professionals. Privacy issues impact all of our professional and personal lives. It is imperative that we educate ourselves about the laws, best practices, and ethical issues related to information privacy to remain relevant in a global economy.

NOTES

1. Secretary's Advisory Committee on Automated Personal Data Systems, "Records, Computers, and the Rights of Citizens," No. (OS) 73-94, U.S. Department of Health, Education and Welfare, 1973, www.justice.gov/opcl/docs/rec-com-rights.pdf.

2. Ibid., xx–xxi.

3. Privacy Act of 1974, 5 U.S.C. § 552a, as amended.

4. "The OECD Privacy Framework," Organisation for Economic Co-Operation and Development, 2013, www.oecd.org/sti/ieconomy/oecd_privacy_framework.pdf.

5. Hugh G. Stevenson, Office of International Affairs, U.S. Federal Trade Commission, "30 Years After: The Impact of the OECD Privacy Guidelines," remarks made at the 30 Years After: The Impact of the OECD Privacy Guidelines conference, Paris, March 10, 2010, www.oecd.org/internet/ieconomy/44946205.pdf.

6. The term *data controller* is used to refer to an organization with the authority to decide how data will be processed. The term is defined in article 2(d) of the European Privacy Directive as "the natural or legal person, public authority, agency or any other body which alone or jointly with others determines the purposes and means of the processing of personal data."

7. Organisation for Economic Co-Operation and Development, *Recommendation of the Council Concerning Guidelines Governing the Protection of Privacy and Transborder Flows*

of Personal Data (2013), the OECD Privacy Framework, www.oecd.org/sti/ieconomy/2013-oecd-privacy-guidelines.pdf.

8. "National Strategy for Trusted Identities in Cyberspace: Enhancing Online Choice, Efficiency, Security, and Privacy," the White House, April 2011, www.whitehouse.gov/sites/default/files/rss_viewer/NSTICstrategy_041511.pdf, appendix A, 45.

9. Ibid., appendix A.

10. Ibid., appendix A.

11. Article 8, "Right to Respect for Private and Family Life," Convention for the Protection of Human Rights and Fundamental Freedoms as amended by Protocols No. 11 and No. 14, Council of Europe, 1950, http://conventions.coe.int/treaty/en/treaties/html/005.htm.

12. Convention for the Protection of Individuals with Regard to Automatic Processing of Personal Data, January 28, 1981, http://conventions.coe.int/Treaty/en/Treaties/Html/108.htm, Article 4, "Duties of the Parties."

13. "EU Member Countries," European Union, http://europa.eu/about-eu/countries/member-countries/index_en.htm (accessed April 20, 2014).

14. *Directive 95/46/EC of the European Parliament and of the Council of 24 October 1995 on the Protection of Individuals with Regard to the Processing of Personal Data and on the Free Movement of Such Data,* http://eur-lex.europa.eu/LexUriServ/LexUriServ.do?uri=CELEX:31995L0046:EN:HTML.

15. "Progress on EU Data Protection Reform Now Irreversible following European Parliament Vote," europa.edu, March 14, 2014, http://europa.eu/rapid/press-release_MEMO-14-186_en.htm.

16. "The New European Data Privacy Regulation and What It Means for Global Privacy and the Internet Industry: A Presentation from European Commission Officials," Congressional Bi-Partisan Privacy Caucus and the Congressional Internet Caucus, Washington, DC, November 19, 2013; keynote panel speakers included Isabelle Falque-Pierrotin, president of the French Data Protection Authority, Commission nationale de l'informatique et des libertés, IAPP Global Privacy Summit, International Association of Privacy Professionals, Washington, DC, March 7, 2014.

17. "U.S.-EU Safe Harbor Overview," http://export.gov/safeharbor/eu/eg_main_018476.asp.

18. "Overview of Binding Corporate Rules," European Commission, July 16, 2013, http://ec.europa.eu/justice/data-protection/document/international-transfers/binding-corporate-rules/index_en.htm.

19. "Model Contracts for the Transfer of Personal Data to Third Countries," European Commission, July 16, 2013, http://ec.europa.eu/justice/data-protection/document/international-transfers/transfer/index_en.htm#h2-1.

20. "Article 29 Working Party," European Commission, August 6, 2013, http://ec.europa.eu/justice/data-protection/article-29/index_en.htm.

21. "APEC Member Economies," Asia-Pacific Economic Corporation, www.apec.org/about-us/about-apec/member-economies.aspx (accessed April 12, 2014).

22. *APEC Privacy Framework,* Singapore, APEC Secretariat, 2005, http://www.worldlii.org/int/other/PrivLRes/2005/4.html.

23. "The Cross Border Privacy Rules System: Promoting Consumer Privacy and Economic Growth across the APEC Region," Asia-Pacific Economic Cooperation, September 25, 2013, www.apec.org/Press/Features/2013/0903_cbpr.aspx.

24. *Constitution Act, 1982, Canadian Charter of Rights and Freedoms,* sections 7 and 8, http://laws-lois.justice.gc.ca/eng/const/page-15.html.

25. "Legal Information Related to the Privacy Act," Office of the Privacy Commissioner of Canada, April 9, 2014, www.priv.gc.ca/leg_c/leg_c_a_e.asp; "Legal Information Related to the PIPEDA," Office of the Privacy Commissioner of Canada, April 9, 2014, www.priv.gc.ca/leg_c/leg_c_p_e.asp.

26. "Legal Information Related to PIPEDA: Privacy Principles," Office of the Privacy Commissioner of Canada, April 16, 2014, www.priv.gc.ca/leg_c/p_principle_e.asp.

27. Ibid.

28. "Frequently Asked Questions on the Commission's Adequacy Finding on the Canadian Personal Information Protection and Electronic Documents Act," European Commission, October 9, 2012, http://ec.europa.eu/justice/policies/privacy/thridcountries/adequacy-faq_en.htm.

29. "About the Office of the Privacy Commissioner," Office of the Privacy Commissioner of Canada, April 8, 2014, www.priv.gc.ca/au-ans/index_e.asp.

30. *Privacy by Design* is a term coined by Dr. Ann Couvkian, former Information and Privacy Commissioner of Ontario, Canada. See "Introduction to Privacy by Design," Information and Privacy Commissioner of Ontario, Canada, April 20, 2014, www.ipc.on.ca/english/Privacy/Introduction-to-PbD. See also "Privacy By Design, PbD," Privacy by Design, April 20, 2014, http://privacybydesign.ca.

31. "Social Smarts: Privacy, the Internet, and You," Office of the Privacy Commissioner of Canada, April 20, 2014, www.priv.gc.ca/youth-jeunes/fs-fi/res/gn_e.pdf.

32. "Office of the Privacy Commissioner*," Office of the Privacy Commissioner of Canada*, April 20, 2014, www.priv.gc.ca/index_e.asp.

BIBLIOGRAPHY

APEC Privacy Framework. Singapore: APEC Secretariat, 2005.

Convention for the Protection of Individuals with Regard to Automatic Processing of Personal Data. January 28, 1981. http://conventions.coe.int/Treaty/en/Treaties/Html/108.htm.

National Strategy for Trusted Identities in Cyberspace: Enhancing Online Choice, Efficiency, Security, and Privacy. The White House, April 2011. www.whitehouse.gov/sites/default/files/rss_viewer/NSTICstrategy_041511.pdf.

Organisation for Economic Co-Operation and Development. *Recommendation of the Council Concerning Guidelines Governing the Protection of Privacy and Transborder Flows of Personal Data (2013)*. The OECD Privacy Framework. www.oecd.org/sti/ieconomy/2013-oecd-privacy-guidelines.pdf.

Glossary

Binding Corporate Rules (BCRs): Binding Corporate Rules (BCRs) are a means by which companies operating in more than one jurisdiction can demonstrate their commitment to adequate safeguards for the protection of the privacy of individuals. They are rules that are legally binding and must be approved by data-protection authorities in the EU member countries in which the companies operate.

Consumer Financial Protection Bureau (CFPB): The CFPB was established by provisions in the Dodd-Frank Wall Street Reform and Consumer Protection Act of 2010. It provides oversight to companies involved in consumer financial products and services. These include banks, credit unions, and financial companies.

Data Breach: The unauthorized access or acquisition of computerized data that compromises or has likely compromised the security, confidentiality, or integrity of information that relates to an identified or identifiable person or persons. Breaches may be intentional or unintentional.

Data Controller: An organization with the authority to decide how data will be processed. The term is defined in article 2(d) of the European Privacy Directive as "the natural or legal person, public authority, agency or any other body which alone or jointly with others determines the purposes and means of the processing of personal data."

Data Mining: Data mining is a process of analyzing data, searching for patterns, and making connections. Data mining is often done with the help of sophisticated software that makes it possible to analyze large volumes of data. Through data mining it is sometimes possible to re-identify individuals whose data had been anonymized. Data mining has been and continues to be used by researchers and businesses. It has been used to identify an individual's online activities and determine buying habits and preferences.

Data Processor: An individual or organization that processes data. The term is defined in article 2(e) of the European Privacy Directive as "a natural or legal person, public authority, agency or any other body which processes personal data on behalf of the controller."

Data Protection: The protection of data, including personal data, from unauthorized access, use, and alteration.

Data Subject: The individual whose personal data is collected.

De-identification: The process of removing identifiers that associate information with a specific individual.

Digital Footprint: A trail of data that remains in the digital environment relating to an individual's interactions. Digital footprints are not limited to the Internet but include an individual's use of mobile phones, cable television, and more. It is a record of what you searched for, looked at, and where you went online. Information from your digital footprint is often used for targeted marketing of products and can be used in background checks.

Fair Information Principles (FIPs): The generally recognized principles of today stem from a 1973 report by the U.S. Department of Health, Education & Welfare's advisory committee on automated personal data systems. It set forth five basic principles concerning information that were widely accepted. The FIPs are at the core of the Privacy Act of 1974. The FIPs were updated and now include eight principles of fair information practice. See "Fair Information Practice Principles" below.

Fair Information Practice Principles (FIPPs): The original FIPs were updated. Eight principles now form the foundation of fair information practice in the United States and expand on the original principles. They are: transparency, individual participation, purpose specification, data minimization, use limitation, data quality and integrity, security, and accountability and auditing.

Federal Communications Commission (FCC): Under the provisions of some federal privacy laws, along with the Federal Trade Commission, the FCC is required to issue regulations. These regulations impose specific compliance requirements on those working within the private sector. When a covered entity fails to adhere to these requirements, these agencies may become involved to provide corrective guidance and enforce the regulations.

Federal Trade Commission (FTC): A key agency enforcing consumer privacy protections as part of its larger focus on consumer protection. It is an independent agency that, under 15 U.S.C. § 45, is empowered to investigate and regulate "unfair and deceptive trade practices" and may bring enforcement actions.

Foreign Intelligence Surveillance Act (FISA): Under FISA the government may conduct electronic surveillance to collect foreign intelligence in the United States. FISA establishes standards for the use of electronic surveillance, and government requests for FISA orders authorizing such surveillance are reviewed by a special court that reviews them in secret.

Freedom of Information Act (FOIA): Provides individuals with a means to request information from the federal government. Under FOIA an individual may request from an executive branch department or agency any information that is not protected from public disclosure by one of nine exemptions or three special law enforcement record exclusions relating to law enforcement and national security.

Genetic Information Nondiscrimination Act (GINA) of 2008: Enacted to protect against genetic discrimination in health insurance and employment, GINA makes it illegal for an insurance company or employer to discriminate against an individual due to a genetic change that may cause the increase of risk of an inherited disorder.

Health Information Technology for Economic and Clinical Health (HI-TECH) Act: Strengthens the civil and criminal penalties for those who do not comply with HIPAA rules.

Health Insurance Portability Act of 1996 (HIPAA): Established a national standard for the protection of health information. Under HIPAA the "privacy rule" addresses how health information may be used and disclosed.

Information Privacy: The right of individuals and organizations to control the collection and sharing of their personal information without consent.

Internet Cookies: Internet cookies are files that are placed on computers that allow web servers to store information used to enhance the user's experience and to collect data.

Internet Protocol Address (IP Address): An IP address is the unique address that is assigned by your Internet service provider (ISP). It indentifies your computer if you are linked directly to the Internet or it identifies your router if you are part of a local area network (LAN). The IP address identifies a specific location where information will be returned. This is necessary for data transfer.

Model Contract: This term is often used in reference to European Union (EU) privacy requirements. A model contract contains standard clauses designed to meet the levels of privacy protection deemed "adequate" by the EU. It is used as means to ensure the flow of personal data from a data controller in the EU or three other participating countries (Norway, Liechtenstein, Iceland) to a data controller or processer in an area not deemed to have adequate protections.

National Security Letters (NSLs): The Federal Bureau of Investigation (FBI) issues NSLs and can use them to demand information that it deems relevant to the gathering of foreign intelligence or the investigation of terrorism. NSLs contain a nondisclosure order, which means that information requested from entities and individuals through these letters must remain clandestine unless successfully challenged and the nondisclosure requirement is lifted.

Opt-In: The requirement that an individual take affirmative action to agree to share personally identifiable information before it is collected or may be used.

Opt-Out: Allows for the sharing of information with third parties unless the individual takes specific action to indicate that he or she does not want their information shared. A person might check a box indicating the desire to opt-out.

Organisation for Economic Co-operation and Development (OECD): An international economic organization comprised of 34 countries whose mission is to promote social and economic well-being through the use of policies. Members include: Australia, Austria, Belgium, Canada, Chile, the Czech Republic, Denmark, Estonia, Finland, France, Germany, Greece, Hungary, Iceland, Ireland, Israel, Italy, Japan, Republic of Korea, Luxembourg, Mexico, Netherlands, New Zealand, Norway, Poland, Portugal, the Slovak Republic, Slovenia, Spain, Sweden, Switzerland, Turkey, the United Kingdom, and the United States.

Organisation for Economic Co-operation and Development (OECD) Guidelines: Developed to prevent violations of the fundamental human right of privacy, the OECD guidelines include eight basic principles concerning the collection and use of personal information that form a widely recognized framework for fair information practices.

Personal Data: Information relating to an identified or identifiable person. What constitutes personal data varies by country. See also "Personally Identifiable Information."

Personal Information: Often referred to as personally identifiable information (PII) in U.S. privacy law or personal data in European privacy law. The term refers to information relating to an identified or identifiable person. What constitutes personal information varies by country. See also "Personal Data" and "Personally Identifiable Information."

Personally Identifiable Information (PII): A term used in privacy law in the United States to refer to personal data. What constitutes PII varies by country. Some countries are more encompassing in their definitions of PII than others. See also "Personal Data."

Privacy Audit: An assessment that focuses on privacy risk. The audit includes evaluation of all privacy policies, procedures, and checklists, as well as provisions in contracts with third parties who may have access to PII. How data flows through an organization is mapped and data handling practices are assessed to determine if they comply with legal requirements and industry best practices. Audits may also focus on compliance, determining how well an organization is following its own policies and procedures.

Privacy by Design: A new approach to privacy that incorporates privacy concerns into all aspects of design. The term was coined by Dr. Ann Cavoukian, former Information and Privacy Commissioner of Ontario, in the 1990s.

Privacy Literacy: A term used here to identify one's level of understanding and awareness of how information is tracked and used, especially in online environments, and how that information can thereby retain or lose its private nature.

Privacy Notice: This is a notice directed to the individuals from whom information will be collected and used by an organization. The privacy notice should describe how the organization collects, uses, and stores personally identifiable information. Consumers rely on the information contained in privacy notices, and organizations are held to the terms of those notices by regulators.

Privacy Policy: A privacy policy is a document that instructs those within an organization on data privacy as it applies to the collection and use of data within the organization. The audience for a privacy policy is employees of an organization. An organization may also use its privacy policy as a form of privacy notice, when that policy is made available to those outside of the organization.

Re-identify: To re-identify information means that you associate previously de-identified information with a person or entity. Data miners are able to analyze certain information from databases, which on their own provide anonymous data, to identify data with specific individuals.

Safe Harbor Certification Program: This program was designed to assist companies in the United States that process personal data from the European Union. It provides the means for organizations to comply with the protection requirements and maintain the privacy and integrity of the personal data that they process. Under the guidance of the U.S. Department of Commerce, U.S. companies can self-certify by adhering to certain principles. At the time of this writing, the European Union approves of this program.

Search Logs: Search logs are a listing of search requests that show what search queries an individual typed into the Internet. They are tied to IP addresses. Companies such as Google have saved these logs and used them for data mining, and examination by law enforcement and government agencies. They can be especially revealing as many people search their own names and the names of friends and relatives.

Self-Regulation: In the United States there are a number of self-regulatory regimes that play a role in governing information privacy practices. Groups or associations provide guidance on accepted privacy practices. Under self-regulation industry groups serve both as the regulators and the regulated.

Sensitive Personal Data: A subset of personally identifiable information (PII). In the United States this includes data that is specifically protected such as social security numbers, identifiable health records, and identifiable financial records.

USA PATRIOT Act: Formally known as the Uniting and Strengthening America by Providing Appropriate Tools Required to Intercept and Obstruct Terrorism (USA PATRIOT ACT) Act of 2001, this act expanded the ability of the government to seek information under administrative subpoenas. The USA PATRIOT Act was signed into law on October 26, 2001, in the wake of the terrorist attacks of September 11th. This Act expanded the powers of law enforcement for surveillance and investigation to deter terrorism. Its enforcement accordingly places limits on information privacy protection.

Index

About the Author

Cherie L. Givens, JD, PhD, CIPP, is a privacy consultant, attorney, and lecturer. She earned her MLIS and JD from Louisiana State University and a PhD in Library, Archival, and Information Studies from the University of British Columbia. Cherie is certified as an information privacy professional (CIPP/US) by the International Association of Privacy Professionals. Her library experience includes holding positions in law, special, and government libraries.

Cherie writes and teaches about privacy law, the First Amendment, information policy, ethics, and youth rights and services. She created and teaches a graduate course on the topic of information privacy. Cherie developed privacy policies and procedures, responded to privacy incidents, and served as privacy point of contact in the library services and content management unit of a federal agency.

Cherie's consulting focuses on the privacy matters of businesses, libraries, and other information environments. Her services include performing training and assessments, drafting policies, developing information risk management strategies, and advising on privacy and information management to create and support the growth of privacy programs.

You can contact Cherie at linkedin.com/in/cheriegivens.